China 1937–38

COMBAT

Chinese Soldier VERSUS Japanese Soldier

Benjamin Lai

Illustrated by Johnny Shumate

OSPREY PUBLISHING
Bloomsbury Publishing Plc
PO Box 883, Oxford, OX1 9PL, UK
1385 Broadway, 5th Floor, New York, NY 10018, USA
E-mail: info@ospreypublishing.com
www.ospreypublishing.com

First published in Great Britain in 2018

A catalogue record for this book is available from the British Library.

ISBN: PB 9781472828200; eBook 9781472828217;
ePDF 9781472828224; XML 9781472828231

18 19 20 21 22   10 9 8 7 6 5 4 3 2 1

Maps by bounford.com
Index by Rob Munro
Typeset by PDQ Digital Media Solutions, Bungay, UK
Printed in Hong Kong through World Print Ltd

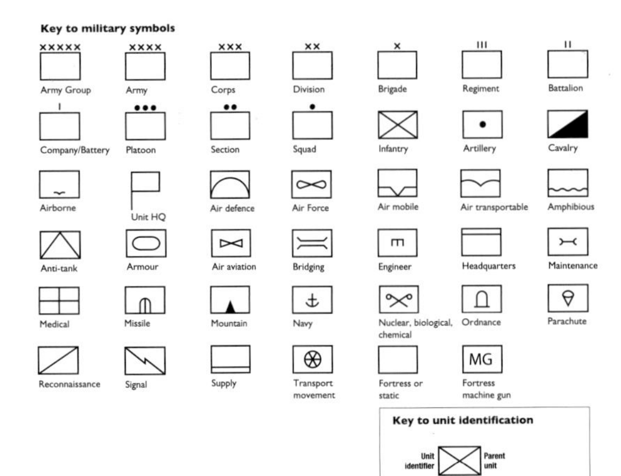

Dedication

To my brother Christopher on his marriage to Mimi.

Author's note

Throughout this book, I have used the Pinyin system, the current UN standard for modern Chinese transliteration. The only exception to the rule is for some key personalities, for whom the name in Giles-Wade or Yale Romanization system is better known: for example, Chiang Kai-shek instead of Jiang Jieshi. In giving Chinese and Japanese names, I follow the Asian naming system where the family name precedes the given name. The names of many of the locations described in this book have changed since the 1930s, but in order for the modern reader to follow the battle more easily, I have chosen modern geographical names over old names, although I have appended the old names for reference.

Abbreviations

2IC	second-in-command
CCAA	Central China Area Army (Japanese army in China, 1937–38)
CCEA	Central China Expedition Army (Japanese army in China, 1938–39)
CCP	Chinese Communist Party
CGA	China Garrison Army (the Japanese army stationed around Beijing and Tianjin)
CO	commanding officer
Col	colonel
CoS	chief-of-staff
Gen	general
GOC	general officer commanding
IJA	Imperial Japanese Army
IJN	Imperial Japanese Navy
KA	Kwantung Army (the Japanese garrison in Manchukuo)
KMT	Kuomintang (China's Nationalist Party)
Lt-Col	lieutenant-colonel
Lt-Gen	lieutenant-general
Maj-Gen	major-general
NA	National Army (Chinese)
NCAA	North China Area Army (Japanese)
OC	officer commanding
PPC	Peace Preservation Corps (Chinese militia)

CONTENTS

Introduction

The Second Sino-Japanese War (1937–45) had its origins in many decades of poor relations between China and Japan that regularly escalated into warfare. Following a series of wars and rebellions in the 19th century, China saw vast tracts of its territory annexed by the Russians. In 1894–95, a newly industrialized Japan soundly defeated China in the First Sino-Japanese War, in which China lost not only its centuries-long hold on Korea, then a tributary state, but for the first time territories such as Taiwan and the Liaodong peninsula. Further humiliations for China followed during the Boxer Rebellion (1899–1901).

Frustrated, the Chinese began to seek ways to recover, replacing the monarchy with a republic in 1911. Civil war among regional factions and warlords ensued; there were two governments, one in the north and one in

The key to the spread of Japanese influence into China before the outbreak of total war in 1937 was through the development of the Japanese-owned Manchu–Japanese Railway. The need for railway security was the excuse for deployment of Japanese troops deep inside Chinese territory. The land on either side of the track was considered to be Japanese territory, not unlike the arrangement made by the Americans over Panama, where lands astride the canal were US territory. Here, in 1931, Japanese troops guard a key railway bridge. (adoc-photos/Corbis via Getty Images)

FAR LEFT
Lt-Gen Zhang Zhi-zhong is shown here in 1933, making a speech at the graduation ceremony of the Whampoa/Central Military Academy. His leadership of the Chinese Army during the 1932 battle of Shanghai aided his rise to national prominence. He wears the modernized uniform of the Chinese Army, with German features such as the ski cap and grey battledress tunic. His rank is displayed on his collar. (Evergreen Photos)

LEFT
During 1937–38, many of the Chinese Army's auxiliary units were equipped with the *dadao*, a machete-like sabre. Paid for by the unit commanders, these swords were of no single design, being made by local artisans. Although the sword was popular in night raids, where surprise was the key, the fact remains that its use in the mid-20th century was a testament to China's weakness and poverty at that time. (ullstein bild/ullstein bild via Getty Images)

the south, but by the late 1920s, Chiang Kai-shek (1887–1975), a military strongman from the southern faction, began to emerge as China's undisputed leader. Even so, many of the regional governors paid only lip-service to Chiang's authority, their stake in the trade in exotic minerals and opium enabling them to build their own power base and protection. Also, the Chinese Communist Party (CCP) grew from humble beginnings in 1921 to become a threat to Chiang's rule. From 1927, the CCP mounted an armed rebellion against Chiang, prompting him to rate the CCP threat greater than that posed by the Japanese and other foreign forces intervening in Chinese affairs.

In 1932, Japan annexed the whole of Manchuria and renamed it Manchukuo, further expanding this puppet state after defeating the Chinese in the battle of Rehe (1933). The real power in Manchukuo was the Kwantung Army (KA), the Japanese garrison. Many long-serving KA officers began to dabble in illicit trade such as opium; flush with funds, some entertained the illusion of being 'independent' from Tokyo. While some extremists began to foment thoughts of coups and assassinations, others repeatedly urged the use of war as the only means to solve the 'China problem'.

Sensing that the Chinese were preoccupied with the Japanese, the Soviets quickly forced the Chinese to give up Mongolia and created a new allied state. The success of Manchukuo led to the creation of more puppet states, including the East Hebei Autonomous Council and the Jicha Political Council; these actions were masterminded entirely by KA officers and had nothing to do with Tokyo. By the mid-1930s, Japanese forces had encircled Beijing except for a narrow corridor in the south-west where the Beijing–Wuhan railway ran. By early 1937, Japan's China Garrison Army (CGA) had Beijing surrounded on three sides, while the KA fielded the equivalent of another eight divisions – 1st, 2nd, 4th, 7th, 8th, 11th and 12th divisions, plus five independent brigades and an air force – supported by a sizeable contingent of local troops. Japan could also draw upon the Korea and Taiwan garrisons (the 19th and 20th divisions). By comparison, the Chinese were

North-eastern China, 1937–38

MAP KEY

In July 1937, the area controlled by Chiang Kai-shek was really quite small. The East Hebei Autonomous Council and the Jicha Political Council were both separatist local councils controlled by the Japanese. At the beginning of what became known as the Marco Polo Bridge Incident, the main force of the China Garrison Army (CGA) was in Tianjin, with outposts in Tong County, Fengtai and along the Manchukuo railway line. In the days before 8 July, the Japanese were exceptionally busy with military exercises, making the Chinese increasingly nervous. After shooting started on the 7th the Chinese reinforced Beijing and the Japanese responded with troops from Korea and Manchukuo.

In the battle of Tai'erzhuang (14 March–8 April 1938), Japan's II Corps, having occupied Jinan, ordered the 10th Division and 5th Division to capture Xuzhou, the headquarters of China's Fifth War Zone. Seeking to link up with II Corps, the Japanese 13th Division was stopped by Chinese forces at the Huai River, and was unable to break through until late May 1938. After Tai'erzhuang, the Japanese attempted to encircle the escaping Chinese, but Japan's 14th Division was caught in the Yellow River flood and the 9th, 3rd and 13th divisions were unsuccessful in trying again to encircle the Chinese fleeing west.

After the fall of Nanjing to Japanese forces on 13 December 1937, the Chinese administrative capital moved to Wuhan. To capture Wuhan, Japan's Central China Expedition Army (CCEA) pushed a southern pincer west along the Yangtze River, while a northern pincer moved south through the Dabie Mountains. The strength of the Chinese effort during the battle of Wanjialing (23 July–17 October 1938) meant that extra Japanese reinforcements were deployed, including the reservists of the 101st and 106th divisions, along with the Hata Detachment.

shackled by the 1933 Tanggu Truce that created a demilitarized zone covering much of northern China. The 1935 He-Umezu Agreement further weakened Chinese sovereignty by forcing the Chinese to appoint a provincial leader known for his suspect loyalty as the garrison commander of Tianjin and Beijing – Gen (2nd Grade) Song Zhe-yuan.

The KA sought to cultivate the local Chinese leaders to rebel against Chiang. Song and Chiang had an uneasy relationship as they had once fought each other during the warlord era. While the Japanese were wooing Song, he retreated to his family home in Shandong province. In 1937, Song was not only the military commander of Beijing and Tianjin, but also the Chairman of the Joint Legislative Committee of Hebei and Chahar Province as well as the head of the Jicha Political Council. Through his subordinates, Song extended his reach into the fabric of northern China.

Even so, the Japanese premier, Hirota Koki, still hoped to find a peaceful solution to the China issue because he believed Japan had to avoid becoming embroiled in a drawn-out war with China while the Soviets posed such a threat. However, the 'hawks' – such as Lt-Gen Tojo Hideki, the KA's CoS who later became the infamous prime minister of wartime Japan – were clamouring for a belligerent solution to the China problem. To counter any moves on Beijing by the KA, Tokyo decided to bolster the CGA with an additional ten companies of infantry and one combined-arms regiment, hoping it could act as a counterweight. Unknown to Tokyo, this force also contained many who shared Tojo's hawkish views – and the Japanese did not forewarn the Chinese of this provocative move, thereby contributing to the increasingly tense atmosphere. Soon after, the enlarged CGA began to conduct exercises using live ammunition and extend its military presence beyond what was permitted by the Boxer Protocol of 1901. A key development was the occupation in 1935 of an old British Army barracks in Fengtai, on the western outskirts of Beijing, only 5km from the strategically important Marco Polo Bridge.

During the Second Sino-Japanese War, the Japanese would win battle after battle, but on the rare occasions when the Chinese were victorious, they prevailed while sustaining a much greater number of casualties. Several factors contributed to this outcome. Not only were the Chinese deficient in key weaponry such as artillery, but also – more importantly – they were short of trained and experienced personnel to operate these weapons. Indeed, by the end of 1936, there were only 17,490 soldiers who had completed secondary education and only 880 who been through tertiary education.

If the average soldier was poorly educated, training staff were little better. Good officers gravitated towards active fighting units that offered better pay and chances for promotion, while the less capable ones were assigned to training units. Many languished in the training establishments for years, holding on to obsolete tactics and doctrine; they failed to appreciate the devastating killing power provided by a few well-placed automatic weapons and continued to promote the closely packed troop formations that so often contributed to the NA's high casualties in 1937–38. It must be remembered that at this time, China was a desperately poor country. One bullet cost the same as 3.5kg of rice or 35 eggs, the cost of ammunition severely restricting training to cover only the most basic of soldiering skills. Poverty forced the Chinese to emphasize classroom education rather than outdoor training.

Although the average soldier's low level of education could be detrimental to the NA's overall fighting effectiveness, under good leadership the NA soldier could perform impressively well. For example, with only one platoon, Gen Sun Lian-zhong, OC 2nd Army Group, was able to defend a key crossroads in Tai'erzhuang against a much stronger foe. This was partly due to Sun, a practical man at heart, alway emphasizing field exercises and plentiful time on the range ahead of theory and time in the classroom.

ABOVE LEFT

In the 1930s, the Chinese Army was far from unified. This soldier probably comes from Guangdong in the south, a region close to Hong Kong, meaning it was influenced by the British in terms of the supply of arms and equipment. (Bettmann/Getty Images)

ABOVE RIGHT

The German-trained and -equipped force was Chiang's pride and joy, but would be largely destroyed during the battle of attrition around Shanghai and Nanjing in the latter part of 1937. In this case, German influence is limited to the helmet and elements of his weaponry – his locally made Mauser rifle and German-style stick grenade. (Photograph by Malcolm Rosholt. Image courtesy of Mei-fei Elrick, Tess Johnston and Historical Photographs of China Project, University of Bristol)

COMBAT

Private first class, 219th Infantry Regiment

This man's parent formation, 29th Corps, was once a northern warlord army, like many provisional armies of the day. In common with many Chinese soldiers of this period, he is probably illiterate, and joined the NA to escape poverty. The son of a farmer, he is in his early twenties, and in reasonable health. His training has been rudimentary, probably conducted by instructors who knew little of the subject; most of his soldiering has been learned on the job.

Marco Polo Bridge, 7 July 1937

Weapons, dress and equipment

This soldier is wearing a locally made tunic (**1**), which had its origins in the Zhongshan suit, a design associated with Dr Sun Yat-sen, the founder of the Chinese republic. The cut and colour varied considerably depending on what was available. While his helmet (**2**) is from British stocks, his firearm is a locally made Hanyang-88 rifle (**3**) with a 39cm bayonet (**4**). Unable to afford leather shoes, most Chinese soldiers of this period wore homemade cloth sandals (**5**).

He wears a cloth bandolier (**6**) with multiple pouches, each holding two five-round ammunition clips. Other personal items include an all-purpose bag (**7**) and a steel water bottle (**8**). Characteristic of Chinese soldiers of this period is the way he carries the two stick grenades, on two cloth pouches (**9**) suspended around his neck. On his back is a scabbard for his locally made scimitar (**10**). Altogether, his weapons and equipment weigh roughly 25kg.

In 1936–37, the Japanese wartime infantry platoon was regulated to field four 15-man sections; three were rifle sections, each with one light machine gun, while one section had four grenade dischargers. There were two men in the platoon HQ, the platoon commander and his platoon sergeant. Here, the gunner is supported by a five-man team: one is the gun No. 2; another, carrying the tripod, is armed with a pistol; three rifle-armed men carry extra ammunition; and the section commander holds a spare barrel. Also pictured are a rifleman who serves as a runner, and a rifleman/chemical-warfare specialist. IJA training emphasized spiritual preparation, long-distance marching and night fighting, and stressed the primacy of the bayonet; unusually, every soldier was taught how to use compasses and maps, but Japanese rifle marksmanship proved to be poor during the conflict. (Central Press/Getty Images)

Japanese

By July 1937 the regular Imperial Japanese Army (IJA), 247,000 strong (aided by roughly 78,000 low-grade Chinese auxiliaries at the start of the war), was still only one-quarter the size of the Chinese NA. IJA forces were organized into 17 regular infantry divisions, one per Army district, plus one Imperial Guard division. These regional districts had to sustain their allocation of manpower through conscription, training and the maintenance of reserves. The exception was the Imperial Guard, the headquarters of which was in Tokyo and which recruited throughout the country. In addition to these 18 regular infantry divisions, there were four tank and 15 air regiments, split into four garrisons: China, Korea, Taiwan and Japan.

The IJA infantry division at this time was in a state of change. In 1936, Tokyo instructed that all 'square' divisions (NA divisions were also 'square') were to be converted into 'triangular' divisions. Varying in size depending upon its role and function but fielding only three infantry regiments, the 'triangular' division was more nimble than the 'square' division, with four. The 'triangular' divisions were divided into three categories: A was the strongest, with 25,000 plus men, followed by B, with 20,000, and C, at 12,000. This change was not entirely accepted, however, and many generals dragged their heels in the implementation process; some 25 per cent refused to change outright and remained as 'square' divisions. The four infantry regiments of a 'square' division were formed into two brigades normally fielding a total of 12 rifle battalions. In peacetime, the division was only 12,000 strong, but – critically – had its own engineers, artillery, medical and transport troops. On mobilization, each infantry battalion gained an additional company from the reserves, adding 12 companies to a division and bringing it to a strength of 25,000 or more. In 1937–38, many of these soldiers from the reserves had completed their two-year military service and then been demobilized before being re-engaged. By the late summer of 1938, however, the IJA would be forced to expand to 34 divisions on account of the worsening situation in the China campaign.

A typical IJA private soldier was conscripted between the ages of 20 and 40 (from the end of 1943, between the ages of 19 and 45), for a two-year term of service, but this was extended to three years at the end of 1938. After this period of regular service, the Japanese soldier was expected to continue to serve in the reserves, first as a 'regular reservist' for five years and four months and then as a 'secondary reservist' for another ten years. After this, he was transferred to a category known as 'First Available Manpower' until he was 40 (extended to 45 as the war continued). Those who passed the conscription test but were not selected for service were pooled into two groups, 'First Supplement' and 'Secondary Supplement', divided according to their fitness level. Before they were discharged, they had to attend 180 days of basic training. These men were liable for call-up duties for 12 years and four months, after which they were transferred to the 'First Available Manpower' category.

Japanese conscripts were generally recruited from the poorer sections of society, but only about one-third were farmers, with another one-third coming from the factories; some Japanese recruits were white-collar professionals or civil servants. Crucially, all Japanese soldiers were literate, products of Japan's mandatory education system. Some 1–2 per cent of the intake were university graduates. In 1937, the rejection rates ran as high as 600 out of 1,000, and high standards were maintained during the early stages of the war. Like their Chinese counterparts, each Japanese regiment tended to recruit from a specific geographical area, furthering the family-like atmosphere within the military unit. Unlike the Chinese, the IJA soldier – at least in the early stages of the war – passed through a rigorous training programme that could last 11 months.

Almost all of the early battles of the war in China were fought by regular soldiers of the IJA, including the first wave of reinforcements that landed in late July 1937. Those who came through Shanghai in late August 1937, though, were mainly reservists – ex-regulars recalled to service. Prior to the outbreak of open warfare in 1937, the Japanese had a very systematic training and recruitment structure that prepared the soldier well for any duties that he might have to face, but so rushed was the mobilization order that many of these reservists did not receive any pre-deployment training to prepare them for battle, so the skills of many were 'rusty' and few were at peak fitness. Here, Japanese soldiers open their 'comfort bags', gift packets prepared by civilians and sent to Japanese soldiers to bolster morale. (ullstein bild/ullstein bild via Getty Images)

COMBAT Private first class, 1st Infantry Regiment

This plate depicts a Japanese section light machine-gunner from the 1st Infantry Regiment, a regular Army unit, part of the Japanese China Garrison Army stationed in the area between Beijing and Tianjin since 1901. Supporting him in the gun team would be the No. 2 and No. 3 team members, whose main job was to carry extra ammunition and tools. In command of this team is the team leader.

Marco Polo Bridge, 7 July 1937

Weapons, dress and equipment

This man is firing the Type 11 light machine gun (**1**), which used the same five-round ammunition clip as the issue rifle. Loading was achieved by dropping up to six clips into a detachable hopper. Lacking a quick-change barrel capability, the Type 11 was very prone to overheating in combat and the open feeder box could collect dirt, resulting in frequent jams.

He wears the Type 5 (1930) uniform (**2**). The key distinguishing marks of this dress are the rank patch (**3**), laid across the shoulder, and the stand-up collar normally bearing the number of his regiment. He is wearing a Type 90 steel helmet (**4**) that is secured via a bow-knot. He wears brown leather hobnail ankle-boots (**5**). Slung across the shoulder and secured by a leather belt is his Type 94 water bottle (**6**), canvas machine-gun tool kit (**7**), 60-round leather ammunition box (**8**) and the leather holster for his Nambu pistol (**9**). A Type 30 bayonet (**10**) completes this soldier's battle order. All told, this kit weighed roughly 30kg.

DOCTRINE, TACTICS AND WEAPONS

Chinese

In the early days of the republic, China sought military guidance from the Soviet Union; later, Chinese leaders looked to Japan for training, but after Manchuria was annexed, China turned to the West for aid. There was no such thing as a common tactical doctrine for the NA. Each warlord had his own preferred approach, much depending on where he bought his weapons. As the head of state, Chiang enjoyed better connections, bringing in German military advisors such as Alexander von Falkenhausen, Johannes Friedrich 'Hans' von Seeckt and Hermann Voigt-Ruscheweyh; these decorated World War I veterans understood that sooner or later China would have to confront a vastly superior Japan, and the only way to fight this asymmetrical battle was to focus upon the use of defensive attrition, trading space for time and drawing the invaders into the Chinese hinterland. Essentially a repeat of the 1916–17 German military doctrine of 'elastic defence-in-depth' but on a grander scale, this differed dramatically from China's previous espousal of a single, inflexible fortified defensive line, which could be broken if sufficient enemy pressure was applied at any given point. An elastic-defence doctrine had multiple lines of less-fortified defences with each protecting the other, weakening the opponent over time rather than overtly seeking to hold back any enemy attempt at advance. In 1938, all the German advisors would be forced to leave China following Japanese pressure upon Nazi Germany.

Prior to July 1937, the NA's experience of combat against Japanese forces was limited to short (but brutal) clashes which resulted in almost every case in a Japanese victory. Chinese industry's inability to manufacture sophisticated weapons, coupled with the financial constraints curtailing China's acquisition of modern weapons in any volume, meant the NA's main tactical doctrine relied upon employing its huge manpower to do the bulk of the fighting. In one sense China's vast population was an asset that enabled the adoption of such extreme tactics, methods the Japanese could never sustain when drawn into a battle of attrition. Outgunned in every respect and lacking long-distance firepower, the Chinese had to accept heavy casualties to close with the enemy, and where possible to choose a battlefield that negated the advantages of long-range weaponry enjoyed by the Japanese. The city fighting in Tai'erzhuang, and the battle of Wanjialing, conducted in highly wooded and mountainous terrain, would demonstrate that this lesson had been learnt by the Chinese. Also, the Chinese had to focus upon attacking the Japanese forces' logistical efforts. The vastness of the country would require the Japanese to use very long supply lines; these would prove vulnerable to hit-and-run tactics conducted by weaker but more mobile local Chinese forces, especially if they had the help of the local population.

In 1937, the best Chinese soldiers were Chiang Kai-shek's Central Army troops, trained and equipped along German lines, under German military advisors. Chiang had planned to reform and re-equip 60 'Germanized' divisions, but by mid-1937 only about 30 such divisions had been upgraded; moreover, many of these did not have the full complement of equipment. Having suffered substantial losses during the fighting in Shanghai and Nanjing, some

Germanized divisions fought in the Tai'erzhuang and Wuhan battles. Conversely, many of the regional troops had their origins in warlords' militias. For such troops there were no tactics to speak of, with a reliance upon sheer weight of numbers. Foreign instruction proved superficial, to say the least, and often the intended meaning was diluted by poor translation.

The NA's lack of artillery was a major disadvantage on the battlefield. While a typical IJA division had 48 field guns, the Chinese division had only 16. In addition, the Chinese had limited stocks of ammunition. For example, in July 1937 the 10th Artillery Regiment, equipped with the German 15cm sFH 18/32L howitzer, had only 200 rounds per gun; once these 200 rounds were gone, new shells had to be imported. By contrast, the IJA's 6th Artillery Brigade landed in Shanghai in 1937 with 48 15cm guns, each with 416 rounds. Chinese deficiency in numbers was compounded by problems with the quality of weapons. For example, except for Chiang's elite Germanized troops, all regional troops had to rely on locally made copies of Western obsolete weapons. The Guangxi 21st Army Group, a provisional formation from south-west China that was badly mauled in the battle of Shanghai (1937), was equipped with Chinese-made artillery with a range of only 915m; Japanese guns could achieve eight times that range, while the Chinese weapons' barrel life was less than half that of the Japanese equivalents. Poor metallurgy was to blame. The third problem was

Nicknamed the 'box cannon' because of its rectangular internal magazine and the fact that it could be holstered in its wooden box-like detachable stock, the Mauser C96 was arguably the most sought-after weapon in China for three decades after 1920. The import model was mostly of 9×19mm calibre, but one local version, manufactured by the Hanyang Munitions Works, had the pistol converted to 7.63mm, while another, the .45 ACP Type 17, was made by an unlicensed arsenal in Shanxi. (© Royal Armouries PR.8647)

This is a posed shot for the benefit of Western journalists during the battle of Shanghai, probably taken in late August 1937. The soldier wearing the German M35 helmet is a member of Chiang's elite Central Army, and the fact that he is equipped with the Mauser C96 means that he is an NCO. The man in the background wears a British-style 'Brodie' helmet; he is probably of Guangdong (Cantonese) origin. (Photograph by Malcolm Rosholt. Image courtesy of Mei-fei Elrick, Tess Johnston and Historical Photographs of China Project, University of Bristol)

The Czechoslovakian ZB vz. 26 was the Chinese Army's standard light machine gun during the war against Japan. Records show that 32,272 were shipped to China during 1927–39, with 17,163 of these procured in 1937–39. The last batch of 100 guns was shipped out in April 1939. The first successful Chinese copy was accomplished by personnel of the Taku Naval Dockyard in 1927, but even these were made from substandard steel and parts were not interchangeable owing to the absence of templates and standard drawings. (© Royal Armouries PR.7226)

that many of the artillery pieces were not used to provide indirect fire because Chinese crews lacked the necessary education and training to perform this role. Furthermore, the Chinese were deficient in spotting equipment such as observation balloons (something the Japanese had in abundance), while Chinese front-line troops lacked the necessary skills and communications equipment to call down artillery fire from afar.

In 1937, China's small armoured force, initially fielding German tanks and armoured cars, was largely destroyed during the battles of Shanghai and Nanjing. When Soviet advisors began to arrive in late 1937, their main contribution was to smarten up the 20th Division, which was upgraded to a fully mechanized formation equipped with Soviet tanks and other vehicles. The arrival in January 1938 of 82 Soviet T-26B tanks and other Soviet military aid saved the Chinese armoured force; later, it was expanded further, becoming

Chinese troops in 1942–43. If the Bren Gun symbolized the British and Commonwealth forces of World War II, the ZB vz. 26 was emblematic of the Chinese effort to defeat the Japanese. The ZB vz. 26 proved so effective that the Japanese copied it as the Type 97 light machine gun. (Keystone/Getty Images)

part of 5th Corps. Joining the Chinese effort in Lanfeng in May 1938, 5th Corps became legendary for its fighting prowess. Even so, the Chinese never had enough tanks; furthermore, inadequate training in specialist warfare such as urban combat and infantry–armour coordination meant whenever the Chinese used tanks, their losses were extremely heavy. This resulted from the Chinese lack of all-arms training, something that they were to benefit from only towards the end of the war, after exposure to US-style tactical doctrine.

In terms of personal weapons, the most commonly seen Chinese small arms were: the 7.92mm Type 24 Zhongzheng or Chiang Kai-shek rifle, a licensed copy of the German Mauser M1924; the 7.92mm Type 88, known as the 'Hanyang-88', a Chinese-made bolt-action rifle based on the German Gewehr 88; and the Mauser C96 'Broomhandle' pistol in various calibres. For automatic weapons, the Chinese favourites were the Czech-made 7.92mm ZB vz.26 light machine gun and the 7.92mm Type 24 heavy machine gun, the latter a copy of the German MG 08. In close-quarter combat, the Chinese could hold their own using a combination of edged weapons, grenades and satchel charges, facilitated by the soldiers' willingness to sacrifice themselves in combat. The use of the grenade or satchel charge was a matter of having a strong arm and knowing how to light a fuse with a match, while the widespread use of the sword as a means of physical education or in traditional martial arts meant that the vast majority of Chinese men grew up with some sort of training in its use.

Japanese

Overwhelmingly committed to the primacy of the offensive, the IJA considered defence to be almost un-Japanese in spirit and practice. The Japanese sought to strike first, believing that a surprise attack carried out with determination would ensure that any campaign would be short and decisive; the fighting spirit of the individual Japanese infantryman, combined with shock actions carried out in surprise, was believed to compensate for a lack of firepower. Junior leaders were not encouraged to think creatively when facing a problem; a failure to capture any objectives was always attributed to a lack of 'aggression' in the application of the plan rather than to the inappropriateness of the plan itself. This tactical thinking would become a serious problem when the IJA came to face better-trained and -equipped opponents than the Chinese as the war progressed.

In the 1920s and early 1930s, Japanese forces were not really tested in China, where the civil war allowed the Japanese to profit from Chinese weakness. The Japanese were able to achieve easy victories, and many IJA officers formed a low opinion of Chinese military capabilities. Through the clever application of diplomatic pressure and the forceful use of military power, the leaders of the Kwantung Army – acting on their own accord without the knowledge of Tokyo – were able to conquer a vast area of north-eastern China without any serious fighting. Similarly, the Marco Polo Bridge Incident would be instigated with personal glory in mind, but this time, the Chinese would fight back, much to the surprise of the Japanese, who concluded that a more forceful application of force would make the Chinese see sense and confer yet more conquered territory upon the Japanese.

This Japanese machine-gun team is equipped with a Type 92 heavy machine gun. The weapon could be fitted with a Type 96 4× optical sight, as shown here, which was mounted directly on top of the receiver. On the left side of the weapon, measuring 33cm from top to bottom, the item with a sweeping curve is the Type 94 5× periscope-style sight. The eyepiece was level with the top of the receiver and was better supported on the sight base unit. (Bettmann/Getty Images)

The IJA envisaged the triangular division as having one unit for a holding attack, one unit for a flanking attack, and the last unit as an exploitation force. Whereas the square division had focused on firepower, the new triangular division fitted the strategy of manoeuvring quickly and destroying the enemy. At the tactical level, the Japanese recognized the following types of attack: the meeting engagement, the hasty attack, the deliberate attack, and the pursuit. The common denominator was the need for manoeuvre as a means to outwit the enemy; this could be carried out before the enemy could build up his defences and in order to catch the enemy by surprise. It might prove better to mount a head-on attack in order to gain or retain the initiative, even while lacking the level of force necessary for the attack.

The meeting engagement was the foundation of all Japanese tactical training. The preference of the day was for the main force to advance in two parallel columns, preceded by an advanced-guard formation that could account for up to one-third of the available strength of the force. The primary mission of this formation was to seize key terrain and destroy roads vital to the enemy, and to launch surprise attacks on enemy units. The regulations warned against delaying action until detailed intelligence could be gathered, instead recommending swift and decisive action.

The deployment of the Japanese main body was covered by available artillery, but on many occasions the desire for speed meant that the infantry did not form up into assembly areas prior to the attack; rather, they went into the attack directly from the march after receiving orders that were usually verbal and very fragmentary. The Japanese expected to mount sharp and aggressive attacks to the front, against key terrain features, and a flanking attack, which had the goal of dividing the enemy into small pockets. The Japanese almost always preferred to attack at night. The aim was to attempt to secure Japanese objectives before first light so that any enemy counter-attack would have to be carried out during daylight, meaning the Japanese could counter the enemy with the support of air power. To aid their attacks the

Japanese showed a marked preference for attacking uphill so that the enemy would be silhouetted against the skyline.

When the Japanese had to conduct retreats and withdrawals they were usually labelled as 'advances to a strategic location'. A characteristic of these 'advances' was that the rearguards tasked with providing cover were usually made up of machine-gun teams that would be sacrificed for the safety of the entire force. Overall, Japanese defensive methods were noted for their rigidity, with the troops involved being willing to die rather than live to fight another day.

The IJA was armed with weaponry vastly superior to anything the Chinese had, both in quantity and quality. Armour-wise, the IJA had a huge number of tanks and tankettes at its disposal. As the early stages of Japanese engagement took place in northern China, an arid area with poor roads and bridges, the Japanese were prompted to develop the world's first air-cooled tank engines and keep the weight of their tanks light. Typical Japanese armour of this period included the Type 97 and Type 89 medium tanks, the Type 94 tankette and the Type 95 *Ha-Go* light tank. Japanese armoured vehicles of this period were very problematic in terms of technical failures, however. There was an institutionalized bias in the Japanese military ethos towards the power of the martial spirit of the Japanese soldier wielding the bayonet. Furthermore, the weakness of the Chinese anti-tank capabilities gave the Japanese armoured units a false sense of superiority.

For the most part, the balance of weaponry fielded by the Japanese proved well suited to the IJA's doctrine. In 1937, the standard IJA rifle was the 6.5mm Type 38 M1905 Arisaka, complemented by the 6.5mm Type 11 light machine gun and the 5cm Type 10 grenade discharger (later replaced by the 5cm Type 89 grenade discharger/light mortar). Before 1935, each IJA rifle platoon fielded four 13-man rifle squads (each with one NCO and 12 riflemen) and two light-machine-gun squads (each with one NCO and seven men equipped with two light machine guns and five rifles). In 1935, each rifle

These Japanese troops are pictured during fighting near the Tianjin–Beijing railway in the last week of July 1937. Note the platoon grenadier at the rear. The mortarman and his No. 2 are setting up a Type 10 or Type 89 grenade discharger. The Type 89 could fire both the Type 91 grenade and the Type 50 incendiary shell, while the Type 10 could only fire a standard Type 91 grenade. The Type 10 had an effective range of 65m and a maximum range of 175m, whereas the Type 89 could reach as far as 620m. (Universal History Archive/ UIG via Getty Images)

This Japanese mortar team is operating a Type 11 infantry mortar, a muzzle-loading weapon with a rifled bore. The weapon was fired by means of a lanyard and had a maximum range of 1,550m. Introduced in 1922, it was the first mortar to be issued to the IJA; a total of 234 units were produced, seeing actions during only the very early stages of the war in China. It was replaced by the Type 92 battalion gun. (The Asahi Shimbun via Getty Images)

platoon lost one rifle squad, instead forming a seven-man grenadier squad equipped with two Type 10 or Type 89 grenade dischargers. This squad was later increased to nine men with a third grenade launcher.

The IJA machine-gun company had four platoons manning a total of eight 6.5mm Type 3 heavy machine guns or its later variant, the 7.7mm Type 92. The battalion-gun platoon had two powerful 7.5cm Type 41 mountain guns (later replaced by the 7.5cm Type 94), providing indirect and direct fire support right up to the front line. In addition, each rifle battalion fielded two 7cm Type 92 infantry howitzers, capable of both high- and low-angle fire. At the regimental level, the IJA infantryman could rely upon four 3.7cm Type 94 anti-tank guns. The most popular artillery pieces used in China at this point were the 7cm Type 92 infantry howitzer (replaced by the 7cm Type 11 infantry mortar in some units), which was akin to a mortar on wheels, and the 7.5cm Type 41 mountain gun.

The 7cm Type 92 battalion gun was a key close-support weapon for the Japanese infantry battalion. This versatile weapon could carry out low-angle direct fire to neutralize fortified positions and machine-gun nests, but could also be used to offer high-angle indirect fire in support. Type 92 guns also saw service in Chinese hands, and were particularly popular with the Communist Chinese, serving well into the 1950s. (Popperfoto/Getty Images)

COMMAND AND CONTROL

Chinese

A key weakness of the NA was the lack of NCOs, so much so that junior officers carried out many of the duties normally undertaken by NCOs in Western armies. Owing to the high attrition rate in 1937–38, the NA would lose almost 10 per cent of its junior leaders; this loss of quality manpower in such a short time led to the rapid depreciation of fighting efficiency. According to a 1938 military report, the NA needed to replenish no fewer than 45,000 junior leaders each year. This attrition of manpower also affected the officer corps. A 1936 American military report reveals that there were 136,474 commissioned officers in the NA: 1,782 were of general grade, while senior officers accounted for 15 per cent with the remaining 83 per cent being junior officers. One of the key problems was that many of these junior officers did not receive appropriate training, let alone specialized trade training. Even in 1945, China could only claim that 64 per cent of the NA's officers had been through some sort of collective training. About one-third came through the ranks. While these made good fighting men by the mere fact that they had survived the trials of combat, they often lacked the command-and-control skills necessary for promotion.

Another issue was the lack of staff officers. Records show that in 1937 there were only 2,000 staff officers in an army of 2 million men; although by 1940 this figure had risen to 4,676, it was still short of the required establishment by some 25 per cent. In 1937, most commanders had to do their own staff work and often those men designated as staff officers were just glorified secretaries. Chinese staff shortcomings meant that many military manoeuvres were not planned adequately, often contributing to chaos and unnecessary casualties. The NA's over-complicated command structure, which required multiple levels of command (in turn requiring duplication of resources and trained human capital to man the organization) contributed to its ineffectiveness during the early stages of the conflict with Japan. The

Two fountain pens can be seen in the top pocket of this Chinese commander, who is taking foreign journalists to the front. The possession of a pen was considered to be a sign of intellectualism and a symbol of wealth, setting this man apart from the rank-and-file soldiers, who were generally illiterate. The vast majority of Chinese senior officers had seen combat, but against Chinese bandits or Communist insurgents, not well-equipped and -trained professional forces such as those fielded by the IJA. The Communists, whom the Nationalists fought continuously in the 1930s, did not have many automatic weapons; certainly they did not have any air power. This meant that NA forces were deficient in basic infantry skills such as camouflage against observation from the air, and light and smoke discipline, contributing to their poor performance in 1937 and much of 1938. (Hulton Archive/Getty Images)

lack of good staff work carried out by competent staff officers to support the decision of the commander meant that the commander often had to base his war plans on incomplete research, thus contributing to poor results.

Lacking radios, the NA conducted long-range communication by telegraph, which was only possible between fixed points and not with an army on the move; telephone networks were also utilized. Battlefield communication relied upon orders and reports written on slips of paper delivered by runners or horsemen. Many commanders did not understand the concept of signal security and by July 1937 the Japanese had broken into much of the Chinese military communications network. Moreover, inter-arms communication was poor or non-existent. Being a predominantly infantry force, the NA never really grasped the concept of the all-arms battle. The few artillery pieces that were deployed in battle were largely used in direct-fire roles, and deployment of multiple guns in concentrated indirect fire as part of battle preparation was rare. Many were deployed in a 'sniping' role, sometimes even just a single gun. It was very much a case of 'shoot and hide', dictated by Japanese air superiority over the battle zones where any concentration of Chinese artillery assets could easily be detected and destroyed before the Chinese could relocate.

Fighting in their own country, the Chinese benefited from local intelligence supplied by patriotic citizens. Battlefield reconnaissance as a part of the preparation of a deliberate attack was poor, however, and incidents where Chinese attacks failed due to poor or non-existent reconnaissance were common. For the vast majority of Chinese forces, cavalry was the principal reconnaissance asset. Even so, the Chinese never had sufficient numbers of military horses for transportation, let alone for use by the cavalry. Whereas the Japanese had built into their infantry divisions a cavalry force for reconnaissance, much of the NA's forces had very few or no horses throughout the conflict.

Japanese

In 1937, the IJA's officer and NCO corps constituted a highly trained force, with many 'blooded' in combat. One key drawback affecting this highly professional force was the fact that the military's position in Japanese society was so strong that there was no counterbalancing force to restrain its more outlandish actions. Japanese overconfidence, combined with the IJA's underestimation of its Chinese opponents, would contribute to failures or unintended consequences that pushed the situation out of Japanese control. The Japanese officers who initiated the Marco Polo Bridge Incident expected the Chinese to capitulate as before. In Tai'erzhuang, the IJA commanders would overstretch their forces, heading deep into the enemy trap, while in Wanjialing, Japanese overconfidence contributed to poor logistics planning, with the IJA forces jettisoning their heavy weapons and mistakenly thinking the Chinese would be outmanoeuvred once more. As noted above, the IJA divisional organization was in a state of transition in 1937–38. The Japanese made extensive use of 'detachments', deploying ad hoc task forces to achieve particular objectives. These would function fairly well in China, not least because most of the sub-units in such groupings served in the same division and had worked together previously.

This picture depicts Japanese close air support in action; this was a force-multiplier which the Japanese possessed and the Chinese did not. Throughout the conflict, the IJA was constantly at loggerheads with the IJN, often over the allocation of resources and matters of prestige. The infighting between the two services was to play a major role in influencing decisions made by the senior Japanese leadership throughout the course of the war. To prevent inter-service bickering, the Japanese high command drew up separate areas of responsibility for the IJA and the IJN. The IJN Air Service operated in southern China and the IJA's aviation in the north. The battle for Wuhan occurred near the Yangtze River, meaning that the IJN claimed an exclusive close air support role. Here, ground troops use flags to aid targeting and prevent a blue-on-blue (friendly fire) incident. (ullstein bild/ullstein bild via Getty Images)

The IJA's officer selection and training procedures were rigorous; in the pre-war years, officer training could continue for years. The potential officer completed a two-year course at junior officer school; upon graduation, he served three months in the ranks before commencing 20 months at senior officer school. After graduation from the latter, he served two months as an NCO before sitting a final commissioning examination. NCO schooling and selection was similar and the training process was just as laborious, requiring mandatory service in the ranks followed by up to two years at an NCO academy. At NCO level, the Japanese valued leadership and personal valour over administrative and battle-management skills, requiring NCOs to demonstrate imagination and take risks in pursuit of victory. As Japanese losses mounted, however, the training regime was cut back and standards were lowered, which hampered efficiency and effectiveness – by 1941, only 36 per cent of field-grade officers were military-academy graduates.

While using telephone networks and telegraph networks like their Chinese opponents, the Japanese also mainly disseminated battlefield orders in the form of written notes carried by runners or dispatch riders. Although the IJA fielded more radio equipment than the Chinese, the sets of the period were large and bulky and only really practical in fixed locations rather than on the move. The Japanese could also use aircraft to deliver messages. All told, the IJA's means of communications were much better and certainly more efficiently used than those of the Chinese.

The Japanese were invaders and thus did not have the benefit of language and local knowledge. They required a network of Chinese collaborators to supply them with information, but because of the Japanese reputation for brutality, they generally did not get much support from the local population. In terms of reconnaissance, the Japanese also used their cavalry for scouting, but enjoyed the additional advantage of information derived from aerial reconnaissance, a luxury denied to most Chinese commanders.

LOGISTICS AND MORALE

Chinese

The typical NA formation moved on foot or if they were lucky by train, whereas a typical IJA division had 200 motor vehicles plus 6,000–7,000 horses. A long approach march could mean that Chinese soldiers were exhausted by the time they entered combat; troops were often committed in a piecemeal fashion that depended upon each unit's march rate, thus reducing their effectiveness. The Chinese lack of air superiority compelled NA forces to eat cold rations for fear of exposure through fires or smoke. Diet varied according to the origins of the soldier's unit: southerners favoured rice as a staple, while northerners had a more wheat-based diet and Sichuan troops enjoyed very spicy food; meat was rare owing to its cost. Chinese support troops were organized on a much smaller scale than those of the Japanese, usually in battalions or companies. Despite these factors, the average Chinese soldier fought bravely, often being willing to fight to the last man.

A key factor for the NA was the issue of national cohesion. Regional commanders who did not owe their rise to power to Chiang sometimes chose to ignore orders, or performed the tasks required of them half-heartedly. Some would even desert their post or withdraw their troops without permission. The destruction of a rival's warlord troops would mean less competition for primacy after the war and thus many of the regional commanders would sometimes hold back their forces when fighting the Japanese – especially when they suspected Chiang's orders could conceal ulterior motives other than the destruction of the Japanese. As the war progressed, this issue became less significant, but in 1937–39 it was a major problem for Chiang. He could be assured of the complete loyalty of the best-equipped elements of the NA, namely 1st, 2nd, 4th, 5th, 13th, 16th and 25th corps, plus the 1st, 4th and 9th divisions – some 380,000 Category One soldiers. In addition, there were 550,000 Category Two troops considered to be of lesser quality and loyalty; the Category Three troops, numbering about 1,070,000, were poorly equipped and notorious for their disloyalty. Deserters were usually shot if caught.

The NA's relationship with the local civilian population was generally good. While there were some who abused their power, the Chinese military on the whole was well supported by the people. Despite the heavy casualties suffered during the early stages of the war, the Chinese military and the civilian population were prepared to fight the Japanese to the bitter end. China was their home and it was fighting for national survival. Instead of breaking the Chinese spirit to fight on, the Japanese military's brutal actions only helped to strengthen the Chinese fighting spirit. Even the Chinese Nationalist and Communist forces, who were fighting a brutal civil war throughout the 1930s, agreed to set aside their differences and join forces against a brutal invader.

Japanese

A typical Japanese division had its own artillery and engineers, as well as plenty of transport, both of the wheeled variety and in the form of mules and horses. Soldiers of the IJA ate rice, vegetables and fish; meat was a rarity. IJA uniforms,

FAR LEFT
An example of Chinese public-relations posters before the Japanese captured Nanjing, the Chinese capital, in December 1937. In this poster, an idealistic Chinese soldier in full German-style uniform and weaponry (plus a sword) is pictured leaping over the Great Wall, leading Chinese forces to victory against the Japanese over the latter's occupation of Manchuria since 1931. The characters read: 'Recover lost territories, relieve our Manchurian countrymen'. (Bettmann/Getty Images)

LEFT
Dated December 1937, this public-relations photograph from a Japanese wartime pictorial magazine shows two Japanese soldiers – a senior NCO (with sword) and a sergeant – interacting with local children for the camera. (Evergreen Photos)

weapons and equipment generally proved equal to the rigours of the Chinese environment, at least at first, before wartime pressures led to a drop in the quality of manufactured items reaching the front. Even so, China was simply too large for Japanese logistics to cope. Proper paved roads were largely confined to urban areas, and long-distance logistics depended upon railways and waterways, which were constantly attacked by the Chinese. The lack of roads encouraged the Japanese to develop armoured cars which could run on railway tracks instead of wheels, while the limitations of China's infrastructure led the Japanese to put the bulk of their logistic burden on pack animals rather than on wheels. The Japanese reliance upon horsepower also affected the development of other weapons systems, best demonstrated by the design of Japanese artillery. All artillery weapons (except for very heavy-calibre siege guns) had to be capable of rapid disassembly, with every component capable of being carried by a horse.

Japanese soldiers were inducted into the IJA on 10 January of each year. To be selected for service was a great honour and those selected bestowed much status on their families. Conversely, in China, soldiers were seen as the lowest of the low; most fathers would never let their daughter marry a soldier. Besides the usual musketry drills and tactical manoeuvres, the key element that set the IJA apart was its emphasis during training upon spiritual and mental hardness. The warrior spirit was central for any Japanese soldier, so much so that the Japanese believed that these intangibles could more than offset any military deficiency or setback.

Japanese combat orders often referred to the 'annihilation' of the enemy, which helps to explain why the IJA had a reputation for cruelty, even killing enemy combatants after they had surrendered. The Japanese had a reputation for extreme brutality. The reservists who came to China in the latter part of 1937 committed the worst sorts of atrocities, such as the Nanjing Massacre. Because of the emphasis placed upon inter-unit competition, many Japanese commanders forced their troops to march in 'light order', relying upon local resources to survive. This behaviour fostered robbery and pillage, thereby poisoning relationships with Chinese civilians. Forced labour, rape and murder were common; instead of subduing the local population through fear, they cultivated Chinese resistance. To suppress this insurrection, the Japanese had to deploy more and more resources to 'keep the peace' as they conquered more and more of China, thus draining resources away from fighting the NA.

The Marco Polo Bridge Incident

7–30 July 1937

BACKGROUND TO BATTLE

To counter the increasingly aggressive Japanese posture around Beijing, the Chinese responded by strengthening their troop numbers in the area. Stationed around Wanping County was the 3rd Battalion, 219th Infantry Regiment (110th Infantry Brigade, 37th Division), commanded by Lt-Col

In July 1937, 29th Corps was the Chinese garrison of the Beijing and Tianjin region. The group of soldiers pictured here are building a sandbagged position at a crossroads in Beijing. The commander of 29th Corps was Gen (2nd Grade) Song Zhe-yuan, a northern warlord general whose loyalty to the central government was tenuous at best. Song's dithering during the early stage of the battle probably contributed to Chinese losses as he did not put his forces on a war footing until well after the Marco Polo Bridge Incident. (ullstein bild/ullstein bild via Getty Images)

ABOVE LEFT

This Japanese soldier is part of the pre-war China garrison. The original caption tells us that he is in Tianjin, a port city in northern China, just 130km from Beijing. Tianjin was the location of the headquarters of Japan's China garrison. He wears the Type 5 (1930) uniform and a Type 92 helmet with Type 99 leather webbing. (© Hulton-Deutsch Collection/CORBIS/Corbis via Getty Images)

ABOVE RIGHT

Col Mutaguchi Renya (with arm outstretched), CO 1st Infantry Regiment during 1936–38, exhibited hawkish and stubborn behaviour that drove the IJA into open warfare by instigating the Marco Polo Bridge Incident of 7 July 1937. (Keystone-France\Gamma-Rapho via Getty Images)

Jin Zhen-zhong. Fielding about 1,400 men, it was a reinforced battalion with two mortar companies – one light and one heavy – as well as an extra heavy-machine-gun company. Wanping County was vital to the Chinese as it commanded the only approaches to Beijing that were not controlled by the Japanese – the Marco Polo road bridge and the neighbouring railway bridge that spanned the Yong-Ding River. Lt-Col Jin sought to anticipate the likely actions of the Japanese; believing that the railway bridge would be their first priority, he placed the 11th Company – his strongest – around the eastern end of the railway bridge and the Dragon King Temple, while the 12th Company was placed at the western end of the railway bridge, along with the heavy mortars. The light mortars and the heavy machine guns were located inside the fortress, with the latter weapons covering an arc of fire stretching from the north-east to the south-east.

From late June 1937, Japanese forces had been carrying out intensive military manoeuvres in the vicinity of the Marco Polo Bridge, almost on a daily basis and during both the day and the night. As a precaution, the Chinese had requested that advance notice be given so that local inhabitants would not be disturbed. To guard against any emergency that might arise during this period of heightening tension, the Chinese increased local defences; Chinese soldiers were engaged in trench-digging and filling sandbags. On the evening of 7 July, however, the 3rd Battalion, 1st Infantry Regiment (7th, 8th and 9th Rifle companies, plus the 3rd Machine Gun Company), commanded by Major Ichiki Kiyonao, would be deployed on a battalion exercise in preparation for an inspection to be held on 10 July. For some reason – whether by design or just forgetfulness – notice was not given to the Chinese.

The Marco Polo Bridge Incident, 7–30 July 1937

MAP KEY

1 0530hrs, 8 July: Supported by armour and artillery, Japanese troops of the 8th and 9th companies, 1st Infantry Regiment attack across the Yong-Ding River, easily overwhelming the Chinese defenders of the 11th Company, 219th Infantry Regiment.

2 Morning, 8 July: Japanese troops occupy the only high ground in the area – Shagang, known as Ichimoji ('Straight line hill') to the Japanese.

3 Afternoon, 8 July: Chinese forces supported by artillery successfully block the IJA at Shaguo Village.

4 Evening, 8 July: After last light, Chinese forces of the 12th Company, 219th Infantry Regiment attempt to flank the Japanese, supported by covering fire from the 9th and 10th companies. The area around the railway lines changes hands several times and despite initial success the Chinese fail to eject the Japanese entirely.

5 13 July: 11th Independent Mixed Brigade (Lt-Gen Suzuki Shigeyasu) moves to eject Chinese forces from northern Beijing.

6 17 July: Having completed clearing Chinese forces from Beijing's northern environs, 1st Independent Mixed Brigade (Maj-Gen Sakai Koji) sweeps across the Yong-Ding River and occupies Changxin-Dian on the afternoon of the 28th.

7 1630hrs, 25 July: Japan's 11th Company, 77th Infantry Regiment arrives at Langfang station unannounced, claiming the need for urgent signals repair. A clash soon erupts, leading to a firefight between the two sides.

8 Evening, 26 July: An attempt by Japan's 2nd Battalion, 2nd Infantry Regiment to enter Beijing through Guangan Gate leads to another skirmish, with Chinese troops of the 1st Battalion, 679th Infantry Regiment (27th Independent Brigade, 132nd Division).

9 28 July: A Japanese detachment (three infantry battalions and one artillery battalion) led by Maj-Gen Takagi Yoshito (20th Division) is rushed to Tianjin to aid the CGA.

10 28 July: Japan's 20th Division attacks the Chinese at Nanyuan, easily capturing Tuanhe. Japanese forces commanded by Maj-Gen Kawabe Masakazu support the attack with armour and artillery while the 2nd Battalion, 2nd Infantry Regiment blocks Chinese elements fleeing east. A party of Chinese senior commanders is ambushed at Great Red Gate.

11 Night of 28/29 July: Four regiments from China's 38th Division leave Beijing.

12 Early morning, 29 July: Chinese survivors from Nanyuan reach Gu'an, Nanyuan having fallen on the evening of 28 July.

13 29 July: After being shelled by the Japanese for refusing to fight, the pro-Japanese East Hebei Peace Preservation Corps stages a mutiny during which 235 Japanese including civilians are killed in an event known as the Tong County Incident.

14 30 July: Elements of Japan's 20th Division move from Fengtai to relieve Sakai's force in Changxin-Dian.

Battlefield environment

The battle occurred in the environs of the ancient cities of Beijing and Tianjin, at the height of a hot dry summer. Like all Chinese cities, Beijing was protected by an ancient city wall, 12m tall rather than the usual 7m. The area outside was sparsely populated open countryside. Other than the 12m-high wall, the only high ground was Shagang, the hill lying between Beijing and Wanping County. Control of this hill allowed all-round observation which was vital to the attacking Japanese. Protected by a 7m-high wall, Wanping County overlooks the ancient Marco Polo Bridge. The wall could stop small-arms fire, but it could not resist sustained artillery bombardment. While the Chinese were hiding behind these ancient defences, the only cover available to the attacking Japanese was provided by small bushes, crops and occasional farm buildings. While these could conceal the Japanese, they offered no protection against artillery and machine-gun fire.

The Chinese barracks in Nanyuan was surrounded by a number of hamlets. These villages were linked by a network of dirt tracks, meaning a cloud of dust would announce the approach of any attacker. As tension grew, the Chinese began to dig trenches to protect sensitive areas, such as the land around the Nanyuan barracks, along with the banks of the Yong-Ding River where the Marco Polo Bridge was located. Because these trenches did not have overhead cover, they offered limited protection against any Japanese indirect fire, perhaps explaining why Chinese casualties were always so much higher.

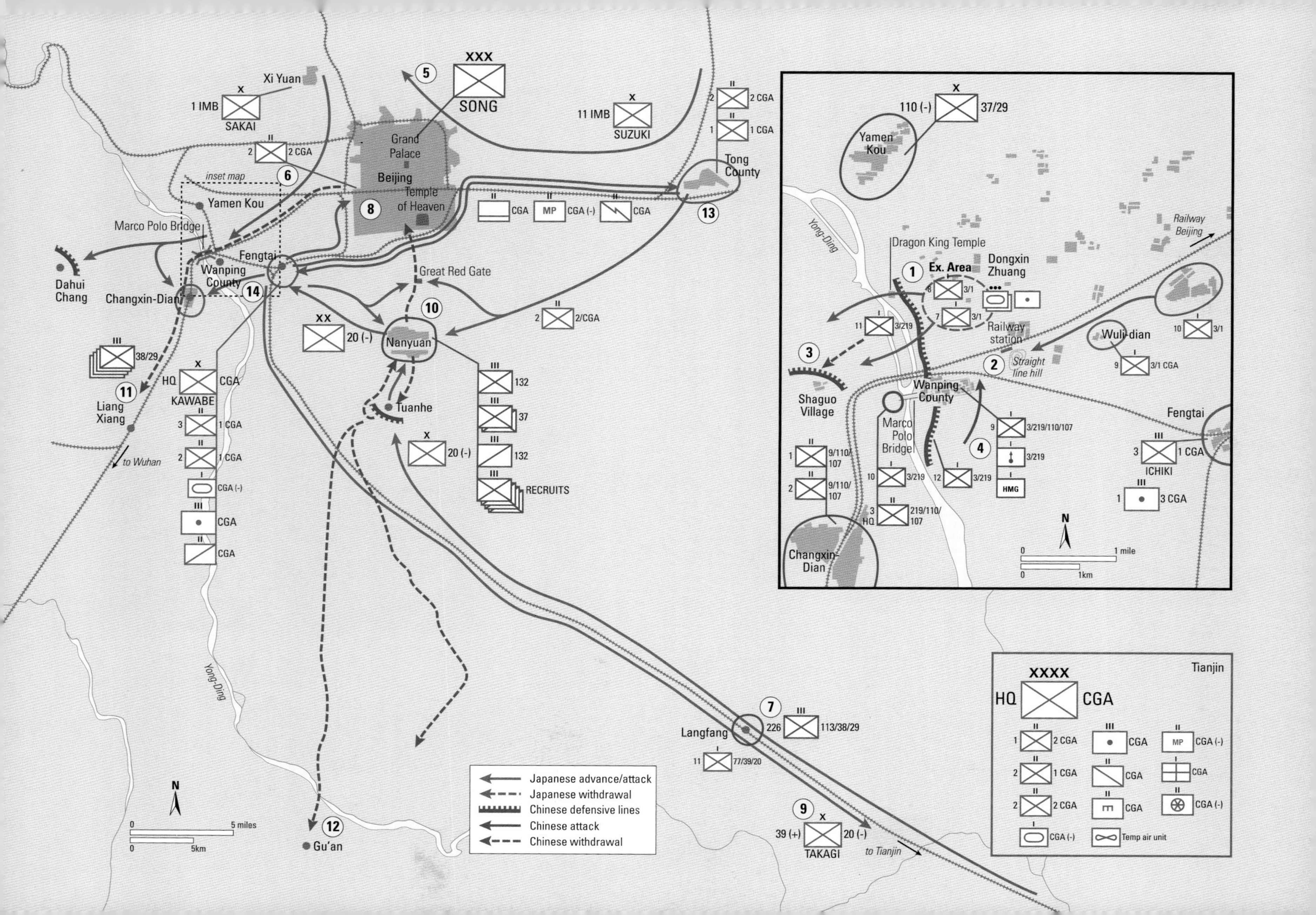

SONG
Xi Yuan
1 IMB
SAKAI
11 IMB
SUZUKI
Grand Palace
Beijing
Temple of Heaven
inset map
Yamen Kou
Marco Polo Bridge
Fengtai
Wanping County
Changxin-Dian
Dahui Chang
Tong County
Great Red Gate
Nanyuan
Tuanhe
Liang Xiang
to Wuhan
KAWABE
RECRUITS
Yong-Ding
Langfang
TAKAGI
to Tianjin
Gu'an
5 miles
5km
Japanese advance/attack
Japanese withdrawal
Chinese defensive lines
Chinese attack
Chinese withdrawal
Dragon King Temple
Ex. Area
Dongxin Zhuang
Railway station
Straight line hill
Wuli-dian
Railway Beijing
Shaguo Village
ICHIKI
HMG
1 mile
1km
Tianjin
HQ
CGA
Temp air unit

INTO COMBAT

Just after 1600hrs on 7 July, Captain Shimizu Setsuro, OC 8th Rifle Company, 1st Infantry Regiment, and his 100-strong force arrived at an area of waste ground just 1km north of the ancient walls of Wanping County, dangerously close to the Chinese garrison. To make the exercise realistic, part of the 3rd Machine Gun Company was to act as 'enemy'. The aim of the exercise was to use the cover of darkness to infiltrate as close as possible to the 'enemy' in preparation for a dawn attack.

Sometime after 2230hrs, Shimizu called a halt to the exercise. The bugle sounded. At first, Shimizu thought that the 'enemy' forces did not get the message that the exercise had been halted, for he continued to hear gunfire, but in his post-incident statement, he claimed that the sound of gunfire was coming from the direction of the Chinese garrison. Other accounts claimed it was just firecrackers, or even agents provocateurs at work. Shimizu saw torchlight flashes from the vicinity of Wanping County which he described as 'signal like'. In the midst of the confusion, the company sergeant-major reported to Shimizu that Private Second Class Shimura Kikujiro, a runner, was missing. Newly enlisted and with less than four months' service, Shimura had last been seen delivering a message to his platoon commander, 2nd Lieutenant Nogei Ichi. As expected, Shimizu reported this to Major Ichiki Kiyonao, the battlaion commander, and soon Col Mutaguchi Renya, the regimental commander, was also notified. Not long after this (some accounts say 20 minutes, others say two hours), Private Shimura returned, claiming that he had a stomach-ache and had to find immediate relief in the darkness, but had got lost. When interviewed on 30 June 1938 by *Asahi Shimbun*, a prominent Japanese newspaper, Major Ichiki admitted that he had been informed of the return of the missing soldier before the outbreak of shooting.

An iconic photograph of the period showing a Chinese soldier of 29th Corps guarding the Marco Polo Bridge, which still stands on the outskirts of Beijing. The men from 29th Corps were characterized by their British-style Brodie helmets and huge scimitars on their backs. (Evergreen Photos)

These Japanese personnel lack helmets, facial camouflage and overhead cover. Three men have binoculars, a sign of Japan being a richer, more industrialized nation than China during the 1930s. (Bettmann/Getty Images)

In the absence of Maj-Gen Kawabe Masakazu, the commander of the CGA Infantry Brigade, who was on an inspection tour, Mutaguchi acted on his own initiative, ordering Ichiki to reinforce the area and pressing the Chinese authorities to allow the Japanese to search for the missing soldier inside Wanping County. At 0130hrs on 8 July a meeting was hurriedly convened by Maj-Gen Hashimoto Gun, the de facto CGA commander as Maj-Gen Tashiro Kanichiro was convalescing in hospital after suffering a heart attack. Knowing the seriousness of the situation, Hashimoto ordered Ichiki to refrain from acting until an official inquiry could be conducted, and instructed Kawabe to head back to Beijing right away. To safeguard his position, Kawabe asked Tokyo for instruction. At 0330hrs, Ichiki was reported to be moving rapidly from Fengtai to Wanping County with the rest of his battalion plus four field guns, two platoons of tanks and an extra machine-gun company. At around 0400hrs, Ichiki arrived at the 8th Company's location with the quick-reaction force. Captain Shimizu immediately informed Ichiki that Private Shimura had been found, but Ichiki was pressed by Mutaguchi to continue to insist on searching for the 'missing' soldier. Soon after Ichiki arrived he ordered Shimizu to move some of his troops to occupy the only piece of high ground in the area – Shagang, known as Ichimoji ('Straight line hill') to the Japanese – to prepare for battle. Lt-Col Jin refused Ichiki's demand, asserting that Japanese troops had no right to enter Wanping County, and reminded the Japanese that it was pointless to search in the dark, saying he would be happy to send a search party in the morning, but Ichiki had his orders from Mutaguchi.

While the tension mounted on the front line, manoeuvring continued behind the scenes. For the Chinese, Lt-Gen Qin De-chun was at the forefront of the negotiations. He refused to allow a company of Japanese to search Wanping County; instead, Qin proposed the setting up of a joint investigative commission, a suggestion readily accepted by Col Matsui Takuro, the garrison liaison officer.

Japanese soldiers wait to go into action, somewhere around Beijing. In the centre is the unit standard-bearer, usually a senior NCO, who was responsible for carrying the regimental colours. The Japanese carried their colours into combat as not only a symbol of unit pride and a prominent rallying point in the midst of battle, but also to stake a claim to 'territory' when the unit captured a key position. The rivalry between IJA units was intense. (Bettmann/Getty Images)

Although diplomatic headway was being made, the situation in the field was deteriorating rapidly. By 0500hrs sporadic exchanges of fire had intensified and by 0530hrs the rest of 3rd Battalion, 1st Infantry Regiment, supported by a machine-gun company, two platoons of armour and artillery, began to move on the Chinese forces defending the railway bridge. As battle commenced, Jin ordered his heavy-mortar company to concentrate their fire on the Japanese tankettes, and the light-mortar unit on the exposed enemy infantry. He then instructed the 9th and 10th companies to provide covering fire while the 12th Company attempted to flank the Japanese. After two hours of combat, although the Chinese managed to eject the Japanese from the railway bridge itself, Japanese forces managed to hold on to the eastern end of the bridge. During the fighting, Lt-Col Jin Zhen-zhong lost part of his left leg and had to retire from the battle.

War had begun, but as it happens the key Chinese commanders – Lt-Gen Feng Zhi-an, GOC 37th Division, and Col Ji Xing-wen, CO 219th Infantry Regiment – were both elsewhere, while Gen (2nd Grade) Song was at home in Shandong province. Fearing Song would reach some form of compromise with the Japanese, Chiang dispatched 15 telegrams to Song urging him not to go to Beijing. In the event, Song travelled not to Beijing but to Tianjin. Knowing that Song was not dependable, as a matter of precaution, Chiang ordered 13th, 26th, 40th and 53rd corps and the 84th Division to move north and dispatched Lt-Gen Xiong Bin, the Military Commission's deputy CoS, to go to see Song (on 22 July) and urge him to remain loyal.

By 1300hrs on 8 July, elements of the 1st Infantry Regiment had taken the Dragon King Temple and began to cross over to the western bank of the Yong-Ding River. When Kawabe arrived back at Fengtai he concurred with the decision made by Mutaguchi, who had arrived at Wanping County in the late afternoon; instead of following Hashimoto's instruction to defuse the situation, however, both hawks encouraged Major Ichiki to attack the Chinese. Further Japanese reinforcements (2nd Battalion, 1st Infantry Regiment, with support from the armoured company, artillery and engineers) were rushed to Wanping County. By nightfall (roughly 1945hrs), using the cover of darkness, Jin selected 150 of his best men to form a raiding party and launched a counter-attack. Armed with small arms, grenades and scimitars, the Chinese managed to recover the lost ground, inflicting over 50 casualties in the Dragon King Temple area alone.

Following this intensive but short-lived battle around the Marco Polo Bridge, the two sides held back from any large-scale attacks while negotiations continued, although both sides sent reinforcements into the area. As the crisis wore on, however, Japanese attention shifted east to Langfang, Guangan Gate and ultimately Nanyuan; at the same time, the Japanese shifted resources away from Wanping County. Even so, brief skirmishes continued throughout this period. Concurrent with the negotiations in Beijing, now that Song had returned, the Chinese Government presented a formal note to the Japanese Embassy, requesting both armies to withdraw to pre-battle positions and for Wanping County to be handed over to the Peace Preservation Corps (PPC). Furthermore, the Chinese invited international mediators to resolve the dispute. As a sign of goodwill, the Chinese began evacuating Wanping County, but the Japanese stood firm. Even so, the Chinese were not unanimously in agreement with Song's decision to withdraw; Lt-Gen Feng Zhi-an, GOC 37th Division, and Lt-Gen Qin, 2IC 29th Corps, were gunning for a fight, but like Song, Maj-Gen Zhang Zi-zhong (GOC 38th Division) was at this stage more inclined to accept the Japanese terms, despite their severity.

To justify war, the hawks in the Japanese General Staff initiated an intelligence estimate stressing the dangers of a large Chinese army in the vicinity. At 2100hrs on 10 July, three hours after the report was written, Prime Minister Prince Konoe Fumimaro was presented with a demand for a general mobilization notice. Among the hawks, the consensus was that

At the beginning of the war, the Chinese fielded several armoured trains. One of these, *Yangtze*, played a minor role in the Marco Polo Bridge Incident. Private Li Wen-lan of the Beijing Garrison's 4th Military Police Battalion recalled that at about 1100hrs on 21 July, while he brought food supplies to the Wanping County garrison, he saw Japanese armour approaching from Fengtai. One vehicle crossed the railway bridge while another moved to the flank, trying to encircle Wanping County. At that moment, *Yangtze* opened fire on the Japanese, prompting the tanks to retire. (AFP/Getty Images)

Ji Xing-wen

Born in Henan province in 1908, Ji Xing-wen joined the local warlord army when he was only 15, probably inspired by his uncle who was also serving in the force. In 1929, Ji was awarded a commission and was appointed as platoon commander. Soon after he applied for a transfer to the cavalry, serving under Gen (2nd Grade) Song Zhe-yuan. Ji was a high-flyer and soon reached the rank of major, finding himself in command of a battalion. In 1933 Ji became an infantry colonel after his excellent performance during the battle of the Great Wall (1 January–31 May 1933). On the evening of 7 July 1937, Ji was the local commander in Wanping County. Because of his tough stance in refusing to bow to Mutaguchi's demands, Ji is remembered as the man who fired the first shot in the Second Sino-Japanese War. By September 1937, Ji commanded a brigade and very soon after was promoted major-general. After 1945, he continued his military career, fighting in the Chinese Civil War (1927–50) on the nationalist side. In 1948 he was seriously wounded during the Huai-hai campaign and was evacuated to Taiwan in 1949 when the nationalists retreated from the Chinese mainland. Ji was killed on 23 August 1958 during the Jinmen (Quemoy) artillery duel with the Chinese communist force.

the Japanese Government needed to impress on Chiang that he should refrain from interfering with settlements being negotiated by field armies. The mobilization plan was approved on the morning of 11 July, but by the evening Maj-Gen Ishiwara Kanji, the KA's deputy CoS, unilaterally cancelled the order and instead scaled down the plan by dispatching only two independent mixed brigades (the 1st and 11th) and six air squadrons from the KA plus one division (the 20th) with three air squadrons from Korea. After a meeting with Emperor Showa (Hirohito) (1901–89) on 14 July, however, the War Ministry dispatched Col Shibayama Kaneshiro on a fact-finding mission, because the Emperor had urged caution. The result of Shibayama's mission confirmed that Hashimoto was right to be cautious. Poor weather delayed Shibayama's return, however, and he was sidetracked by a trip to Korea, only arriving in Tokyo on 20 July just as the hawks in Tokyo managed to enlarge the partial mobilization order to include three Japan-based regular divisions (the 5th, 6th and 10th; these did not arrive in China until August) plus an additional 18 air squadrons. In hindsight, it seems the hawks had it all planned, for even before the mobilization order was issued, warning orders were distributed as early as 8 July, only hours after the shooting started. The 20th Division (Lt-Gen Kawagishi Bunzaburo) duly arrived in Tianjin on 20 July, with the 11th Independent Mixed Brigade (Lt-Gen Suzuki Shigeyasu) and 1st Independent Mixed Brigade (Maj-Gen Sakai Koji) poised at Miyun, a key railway junction some 45km north-east of Beijing.

At 1630hrs on 25 July, 11th Company, 77th Infantry Regiment (38th Brigade, 20th Division) arrived at Langfang station, halfway between Bejing and Tianjin. Guarding the station were elements of the 226th Infantry Regiment (113th Infantry Brigade, 38th Division), commanded by Col Cui Zheng-lun. The Japanese demanded access to the area for the purpose of checking the communication cables. In the absence of Maj-Gen Zhang, Maj-Gen Li Wen-tian, acting 2IC 38th Division after Lt-Gen Wang was wounded, ordered Cui to prevent the Japanese from exiting the station, but to use only peaceful means. By nightfall, it was evident that Cui was unable to contain the situation. The Japanese were digging trenches everywhere, and

OPPOSITE
This unlucky Chinese soldier was one of the many caught in the ambush laid by the Japanese as the Chinese were trying to escape from Nanyuan towards Beijing. He was probably trying to take cover using the truck as a shield, but was caught in a hail of bullets. Note the soft canvas shoes he is wearing – the typical style of footwear of the day – and the half-undone puttees that have unwound thus exposing his calf. In Nanyuan, the Chinese simply had no means to counter the Japanese aircraft and armour. While attacking tanks with grenades was possible when fighting in urban areas offering plenty of cover to infantrymen, the Chinese knew there was no realistic hope of getting close enough to the tanks when they were operating in the open, unless they were prepared to allow the tanks to roll over their positions and then lob grenades onto their rear engine grilles as they advanced – a suicidal prospect. (Paul Popper/Popperfoto/Getty Images)

Mutaguchi Renya

Born in 1888, Mutaguchi Renya was CO 1st Infantry Regiment on the evening of 7 July 1937. Mutaguchi graduated from the IJA Academy in 1910. His early military service took him to Siberia, fighting against the Bolsheviks; later he travelled to France, serving as military attaché. Mutaguchi swiftly ascended the promotion ladder, by 1930 reaching the rank of colonel. In 1933–36 he served as a staff officer in Tokyo, before being transferred to Beijing to take command of the 1st Infantry Regiment. Despite his insubordination while instigating a war without authorization, Mutaguchi was promoted to Maj-Gen in 1938 and served as chief-of-staff of the Fourth Army. Mutaguchi's finest hour was when he was GOC 18th Division during the invasion of Malaya and the battle of Singapore (1941–42), but he was to fall from grace in the battle of Imphal (8 March–3 July 1944), where his dismal performance saw him relegated to the reserves. Because of his stupidity Japan lost more soldiers to hunger and nutrition-related disease than from combat with the British. He was arrested in 1945 for war crimes committed in Singapore, but was later released. After World War II, Mutaguchi made a living as a restaurateur in Tokyo before passing away in 1966, aged 78.

so he decided to employ more forceful means. The Chinese decided to lay an ambush, catching the Japanese unprepared, and soon managed to gain the upper hand. By daybreak, however, Japanese air power and extra troops arrived and the Chinese were forced to withdraw.

At this moment, news of the fighting in Beijing removed any last chance for peace. On the evening of 26 July, a convoy of 26 trucks, carrying 500 men from the 2nd Battalion, 2nd Infantry Regiment, and escorted by two Type 94 tankettes, tried to enter Beijing via Guangan Gate. The Japanese claimed that they were embassy guards returning from a military exercise. Knowing it was a ruse, Col Liu Ru-zhen, OC 2nd Infantry Regiment, decided to act. On gate-guard duty was the 1st Battalion, 679th Infantry Regiment (27th Independent Brigade, placed under command of the 132nd Division). The Chinese allowed the first group of vehicles to enter before shutting the gate and thereby cutting the Japanese force in two. The Chinese rained gunfire and grenades on the trapped Japanese, while the Japanese force on the outside was soon surrounded by Chinese reinforcements. By 2130hrs, negotiations resulted in a proposal according to which the Japanese already inside the gate

would proceed to the embassy and the Japanese left outside would head back to Fengtai. The Japanese lost two dead and 17 wounded, while the Chinese captured three heavy trucks and five cars, plus ammunition and mortars; both Japanese tankettes were destroyed.

By the end of 26 July, all hopes of peace were gone. The CGA issued a demand to the Chinese to withdraw from Beijing and Wanping County. The demand was soundly rejected by Song, who began redeploying his troops and prepared to attack on 1 August. As it turned out, though, Lt-Gen Katsuki Kiyoshi, Tashiro's successor as CGA commander (Tashiro had died on 16 July), would be quicker off the mark thanks to information from Chinese traitors. The Japanese attack was brought forward to 1500hrs on 27 July and the target was Nanyuan, the main barracks of 29th Corps, located 15km south of Beijing.

Lt-Gen Zhao Deng-yu was appointed as commander of Nanyuan. First came a series of probing Japanese attacks on the outskirts of Tuanhe, 6km south of Nanyuan, forcing Chinese cavalry to withdraw, but the main Japanese strike was launched at 0530hrs on 28 July with the support of the CGA's armour company – principally armed with the Type 89 medium tank and the Type 94 tankette – and aircraft. The 20th Division was to attack from the south while the 2nd Battalion, 1st Infantry Regiment would attack from the north-west, having formed up behind the dyke by Panjia Temple, some 7km from Nanyuan barracks. To deny the Chinese any means of escape, the

Japanese troops celebrate victory in Fengtai barracks, on the outskirts of Beijing, during the Marco Polo Bridge Incident. These Japanese troops are carrying a 'good luck flag'. Known in Japanese as *hinomaru*, this was a traditional gift for Japanese servicemen deployed in overseas campaigns and was signed by friends and relatives wishing for the soldiers' safe return. In return, the Japanese soldiers would send a few strands of their hair and fingernail clippings to their families as mementoes, in case they did not come back alive. If a deceased soldier's body was lost, these vestiges of the dead could be used by grieving relatives to hold a funeral. (ullstein bild/ullstein bild via Getty Images)

A group of Japanese soldiers celebrate victory in Tianjin after driving the Chinese 29th Corps out of northern China. At an early stage, the IJA demonstrated its understanding of propaganda by allowing selected journalists to be embedded with the troops, thus giving some media outlets unique access to news from the front. By contrast, the Chinese, being a poorer nation, did not have so many photographers; many of the pictures of Chinese forces during this period were taken by Western journalists, and only after late 1938 did the Chinese manage to mobilize their propaganda machine. (ullstein bild/ullstein bild via Getty Images)

CGA's armoured assets were positioned so they cut the road to Beijing. A lucky hit from the air managed to strike the Chinese headquarters, killing most of the command staff and leaving the Chinese troops without direction, quickly leading to panic in the face of the 20th Division's determined attacks. Without any means to counter the Japanese armour and aircraft, Chinese troops began to flee.

The Japanese attack on Nanyuan was a classic 'hammer and anvil' action where the push from the south, led by armour, punched through the Chinese defences while a blocking force moved from the west and the east, thereby denying the Chinese troops any possibility of escaping to the north. While the southern Japanese force was made up of a mixture of infantry and armour, the blocking force was principally infantry, supported by infantry guns and heavy machine guns. Many of the Chinese soldiers in Nanyuan were recruits, some being student cadets with little or no training who were tasked with defending the barracks. They were deployed in hastily dug open trenches with no overhead cover; when they found they were facing Japanese armour – with the majority having never seen such vehicles before – many of these 'student' soldiers broke and ran.

At 0925hrs, Lt-Gen Suzuki Shigeyasu, the commander of the 11th Independent Mixed Brigade who was perched on a roof directing gunfire, observed a dust cloud moving north and concluded that it must be the Chinese trying to escape. The 3rd Battalion, 1st Infantry Regiment, which by this point was just outside the north-western corner of Nanyuan barracks, was immediately directed to cut off the Chinese retreat. At about 1015hrs, the Chinese were spotted moving up the road; they were walking into an ambush. First to break were the inexperienced cadets, then the cavalry; both were cut down to the last man. By this time, the Japanese had been reinforced by a number of heavy machine guns. The departure of the Chinese from Nanyuan was leaked to the Japanese by Chinese traitors of 29th Corps. At 1245hrs, the Japanese spotted cars coming up the road. Col Dong Sheng-tang, GOC 114th Infantry Brigade (38th Division), later recalled that, having received orders to withdraw, three senior Chinese officers – Lt-Gen Tong Lin-ge (2IC 29th Corps), Lt-Gen Zhao Deng-yu (GOC 132nd Division) and Lt-Gen Wang Xi-ding (2IC 38th Division) – were heading north by car when they were ambushed at Great Red Gate. With their vehicles' progress hindered by the dead horses littering the road and with the Japanese only 60m away, the party was cut down; of the three, only Wang survived. Dong and the rest of the surviving Chinese troops fought it out until dusk, when they attempted a break-out. By the time they reached Gu'an on 29 July, Dong's force numbered only 3,800, over 5,000 having been lost.

On 27 July, while the 20th Division was attacking Nanyuan from the south, the 1st and 11th Independent Mixed brigades swept south and captured Qinghe Town and Shahe, 30km north-north-west from the centre of Beijing. Suzuki's 11th Independent Mixed Brigade then went on to capture Beijing, while Sakai's 1st Independent Mixed Brigade moved west towards the Marco Polo Bridge. By 29 July the Chinese had been outmanoeuvred, and Beijing surrendered without firing a shot.

While the battle raged around Beijing, Tianjin was totally quiet. Just as Maj-Gen Li Wen-tian was deciding what to do, shooting started at Langfang on 25 July; Li decided not to wait for instructions and opted to launch a pre-emptive strike on the Japanese garrison in Tianjin at dawn on 29 July. Li divided his force into three. Using the cover of darkness, one element attacked towards Haiguang Temple, where the Japanese main barracks were located; a second force was to capture the eastern railway station, including a military warehouse; and a third attacked the main railway station. At that time many of the Japanese soldiers in Tianjin were rear-echelon support troops, meaning that the Chinese easily captured both the railway stations; owing to the barracks' strong defences and the Chinese lack of artillery, though, the barracks remained in Japanese hands. Under pressure, the Japanese ordered a detachment led by Maj-Gen Takagi Yoshito (39th Brigade, 20th Division) to reinforce Tianjin. One PPC detachment successfully infiltrated the Japanese airfield at Dongjuzi and torched ten aircraft before the rest managed to take off. Once in the air these aircraft bombed and strafed the Chinese without encountering any opposition, for there were no anti-aircraft weapons available. Japanese reinforcements poured in, and the superior firepower of the Japanese forced the Chinese to withdraw from Tianjin. By late on 30 July, Tianjin was in the hands of the Japanese; Wanping County was also taken, this marking the end of the Marco Polo Bridge Incident.

Tai'erzhuang

14 March–8 April 1938

BACKGROUND TO BATTLE

By December 1937, the Japanese capture of Beijing and Tianjin had been complemented by success on the Shanghai–Nanjing front, culminating in the destruction of Chiang's German-trained and -equipped Army, and the capture of China's capital. To the dismay of the Japanese, however, the Chinese did not surrender after the fall of Nanjing; instead, its loss seemed to fire the Chinese determination to fight on, regardless of casualties. By January 1938, the mood had changed completely. Having expanded from the original 17 divisions to 24 and with 21 divisions already committed in the China campaign, the Japanese armies on the ground seemed to be striking east, west and in every direction without a master plan, and there were never enough troops. In order to stabilize the situation and replenish the Japanese forces in the face of increasing losses, the war council met on 16 February, presided over by the Emperor himself, and announced a one-year hiatus in

Throughout the whole of the Second Sino-Japanese War, the IJA relied heavily on pack animals for transportation. The NA of the same period was in an even more basic state, most transportation relying upon man-packs and pushcarts. To cater for the large numbers of animals employed, the IJA incorporated a very comprehensive veterinarian team in each division. By contrast, the NA lacked such specialist units. (Popperfoto/Getty Images)

Rail travel was the commonest method of long-distance transportation in 1930s China, which had notoriously poor-quality roads at the time. This meant that capturing and holding on to railway assets played a vital role in winning or losing battles. Here, a group of Japanese train guards have been compelled to travel on the roof of a troop train as a means of heading off regular Chinese attacks on the railway. Note the *tabi* shoes on the backpack; the *tabi* was a split-toe high-leg shoe with a canvas top and a rubber sole, used by generations of Japanese rickshaw-pullers. (Walter Bosshard/ullstein bild via Getty Images)

further military operations in China. To ensure that the generals in the field would toe the line, the General Staff dispatched Col Kawabe Torashiro as a representative to deliver the council decision; the generals, though, would have none of it, and Kawabe was humiliated and sent packing.

Despite having the plan rejected by the General Staff, an element of the southern force – 13th Division, led by Lt-Gen Ogisu Rippei – continued to drive north across the Yangtze River and try to marry up with a part of the northern force driving south. In the meantime, the northern force split itself into three. One part – including the 5th Division and the 1st, 2nd, 11th and 15th Independent Mixed brigades, plus Mongolian forces – drove west, using the railway as an axis of advance to take Zhang-Jia-Kou and Datong, in the Pingsui railway campaign. A second force – I Corps (Lt-Gen

These heavily laden Japanese troops can be identified as soldiers of the support company because they carry boxes of ammunition on their backs. They could be serving in the field-gun troop or they could be carrying ball ammunition for a heavy machine gun, which in 1937 was the Type 3 or the Type 92, both being copies of the French Hotchkiss machine gun. For the most part, Japanese troops of the 1930s depended upon pack animals – or in this case, human muscle. The poor quality of roads in China meant that motor transport did not give the Japanese much of an advantage over the Chinese. (Heinrich Hoffmann/ullstein bild via Getty Images)

In 1934, the Germans supplied the Chinese with the drawings for the Maxim sMG 08 heavy machine gun to facilitate local production; designated the Type 24 heavy machine gun, the Chinese version was made at Jinling Arsenal in Nanjing. From 1929, all weapons built at Jinling Arsenal (the sole maker of the Type 24) could be identified by a reverse swastika, an ancient Buddhist symbol. China's main infantry-support weapon during the Second Sino-Japanese War, the Type 24 chambered the 7.92×57mm Mauser round, the standard military rifle cartridge of Nationalist China. When aiming at ground targets, it was usually fitted with a muzzle disc. When used as an anti-aircraft gun, a metal pedestal was employed to raise the tripod and the muzzle disc was usually omitted. (© Royal Armouries PR.257)

Katsuki Kiyoshi) – was to drive south-west from the Marco Polo Bridge along the Beijing–Wuhan railway to Taiyuan via Shi-Jia-Zhuang, in the Taiyuan campaign. A third force – II Corps (Lt-Gen Nishio Toshizo) – was divided into two columns; it was to drive south along the Tianjin–Cangzhou railway line, passing Jinan, the capital of Shandong province, and eventually reach Xuzhou, known as Tongshan/Tungshan or Copper Mountain by the Japanese. This third force sought to link up with the 13th Division, which was fighting northwards along the Beijing–Wuhan railway. The capture of Xuzhou was critical to the Japanese not only because it was where the north–south and east–west railways converged, but also because it was a vital staging post on the Grand Canal. Furthermore, Xuzhou would be a perfect launching pad for an attack on Wuhan. To capture Xuzhou, it was deemed necessary to take Tai'erzhuang, which lies just north of Xuzhou; Tai'erzhuang was a key transportation hub and also the headquarters of China's Fifth War Zone.

A Type 24 heavy machine gun in action. Like the original sMG 08, it required a crew of four. The lack of automatic weapons was a major handicap for the Chinese. Towards the end of World War I, a typical German infantry division had about 108 heavy and 216 light machine guns, whereas in the early days of the Second Sino-Japanese War, China's scale of issue was about 30 per cent that of the Germans'. (Evergreen Photos)

The road to Tai'erzhuang, 16 February–8 April 1938

MAP KEY

1 16 February: Despite being ordered by Tokyo to cease offensive operations, Lt-Gen Nishio Toshizo, GOC II Corps, nevertheless authorizes the 10th Division to clear Chinese forces east of the Grand Canal, supporting the 5th Division in a parallel action along the Yi River.

2 20 February: The Nagase Detachment (Maj-Gen Nagase Takehira) successfully displaces the Chinese from Jining and occupies Jiaxiang on 25 February despite counter-attacks by the 22nd and 127th divisions.

3 22 February: Chinese forces halt the advance of the Katano Detachment (Col Katano Teiken) at Ju County. The Sakamoto Detachment (Maj-Gen Sakamoto Jun) is ordered to 'rescue' Katano, but 40th Corps and 59th Corps counter-attack and repel the Japanese until the IJA unleashes air power that halts the Chinese counter-attack.

4 23 February: Maj-Gen Seya Hajime is ordered to lead a reinforced brigade group (the Seya Detachment) towards Yi County, but encounters heavy resistance from 22nd Corps around Teng County. Seya captures Teng County (17 March), Lin City (17 March) and Hanzhuang (19 March). The Japanese left-flank force moves east to Zaozhuang to support the Sakamoto Detachment, but is itself trapped (25 March) in Guoliji, just east of Zaozhuang.

5 24 March: Despite breaching the wall of Tai'erzhuang, the Seya Detachment is unable to capture the ancient town despite being supported by the Sakamoto Detachment from the east.

6 2 April: Attacking from the west and fielding 150mm artillery, the 20th Army Group (Lt-Gen Tang En-bo), supported by the 2nd Army Group from the south-west and south-east, breaks Seya's force in its staging area just north of Tai'erzhuang. The Seya Detachment is trapped, but is able to break out on 5 April – albeit with substantial losses.

Battlefield environment

In 1938, Tai'erzhuang was a small town of approximately 5,000 families housed in some 20,000 buildings. Protected by an ancient city wall as well as a moat, the town served as a way station for boatmen and traders moving along the Grand Canal. The town itself was not large, being crossed by only eight main streets, but leading off from these main thoroughfares were 437 small lanes and alleys that crisscrossed the town. The narrowness of these alleyways would prevent the Japanese deploying their tanks during the battle.

To the north of Tai'erzhuang were a series of hamlets and villages linked by dirt tracks and cobbled highways. The battle took place early in the growing season; the crops had yet to mature. The lack of heavy vegetation that could block lines of sight proved to be an important advantage for the Japanese, with their long-range weapons.

Teng County was another ancient walled town. On the approach to Teng County, the land became quite hilly, and many of these hills were covered with boulders and woods, offering the Chinese ideal points from which to stage an ambush. To the east was the Lin River, more than 300m wide through the area of the battle and at its broadest 1.5km wide, forming a natural barrier for both armies.

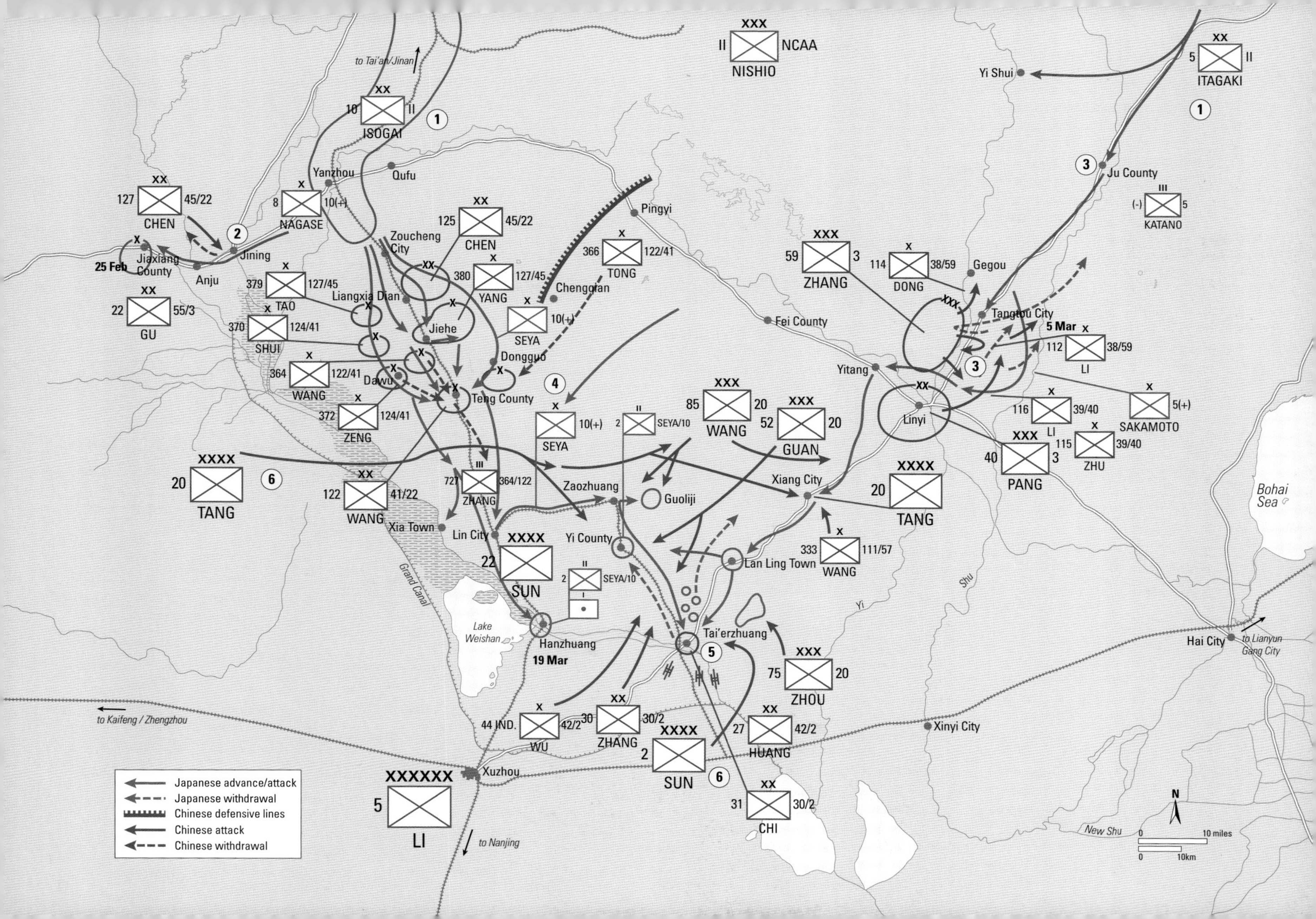

NISHIO
ITAGAKI
Yi Shui
Ju County
KATANO
ISOGAI
to Tai'an/Jinan
Yanzhou
Qufu
NAGASE
CHEN
Jining
Jiaxiang County
25 Feb
Anju
GU
Zoucheng City
Pingyi
TONG
Chengqian
TAO
YANG
Liangxia Dian
SHUI
Jiehe
SEYA
Dongguo
WANG
Dawu
Teng County
ZENG
ZHANG
DONG
Gegou
Tangtou City
5 Mar
LI
Fei County
Yitang
Linyi
SAKAMOTO
ZHU
PANG
GUAN
Xiang City
TANG
Bohai Sea
Zaozhuang
Guoliji
SEYA/10
Yi County
Lin City
Xia Town
SUN
Grand Canal
Lake Weishan
Hanzhuang
19 Mar
Lan Ling Town
Tai'erzhuang
ZHOU
Shu
Yi
Hai City
to Lianyun Gang City
to Kaifeng / Zhengzhou
44 IND.
WU
HUANG
Xinyi City
Xuzhou
to Nanjing
CHI
New Shu
10 miles
10km
Japanese advance/attack
Japanese withdrawal
Chinese defensive lines
Chinese attack
Chinese withdrawal

INTO COMBAT

After participating in the Shanghai–Nanjing campaign, Lt-Gen Ogisu Rippei split his heavily reinforced 13th Division into three columns on 28 January 1938 and continued moving north-west towards Xuzhou. The intermediate Japanese objective was Bengbu, a major town due south of Xuzhou. Ogisu's progress was blocked by dogged Chinese resistance, however, initially conducted by 31st and 7th corps, which successfully completed a reserve bridge demolition and withdrew across the Huai River. 51st Corps strove to counter the Japanese effort to cross the Huai. After mounting a stout defence, the exhausted troops of 51st Corps withdrew and were replaced on 12–13 February with 59th Corps, now led by Lt-Gen Zhang Zi-zhong, the former mayor of Tianjin who had narrowly evaded capture after that city's fall. In late January and early February the 24th Army Group employed 48th, 7th and 31st corps to conduct hit-and-run attacks that targeted the rear of Ogisu's 13th Division, which also faced a series of determined counter-attacks mounted by Zhang's 59th Corps. Under sustained attack over a period of five months, the 13th Division never did manage to cross the Huai. By March 1938, after the line was stabilized, 51st and 59th corps were withdrawn to Xuzhou and the defence of the Huai was handed back to the now revitalized 31st Corps.

Meanwhile, to the north, Gen Count Terauchi Hisaichi led the North China Area Army (NCAA), as the northern Japanese force was known after 21 August 1937. Terauchi deployed two corps: I Corps (Lt-Gen Katsuki Kiyoshi), which participated in the Taiyuan campaign, and II Corps (Lt-Gen Nishio Toshizo), which became embroiled in the rush to capture Xuzhou. Nishio decided to deploy his two divisions in a giant pincer movement: the 5th Division (Lt-Gen Itagaki Seishiro) formed the easterly prong, while the 10th Division (Lt-Gen Isogai Rensuke) formed the westerly prong.

The 5th Division had an easy start to its southern expedition. On 10 January, Qingdao fell without IJA forces having to lift a finger, as the IJN pre-empted the IJA move and took the city. Moreover, Gen (2nd Grade) Han Fu-ju, the military governor of Shandong province and 2IC Fifth War Zone, had abandoned his position and let Itagaki's men take Jinan, the provincial capital, on 26 December, thus allowing the Japanese to breach the Yellow River defensive line without having to fire a shot. Han and many of his subordinates were later arrested and Han himself was executed on Chiang's personal command. This act stunned the notoriously rebellious NA and from then onwards its discipline improved significantly.

As the Japanese advanced further south, their exposed rear-echelon supply train became increasingly inviting to the Chinese. Gen (1st Grade) Li Zong-ren, GOC Fifth War Zone, ordered the 3rd Army Group (Gen (2nd Grade) Yu Xue-zhong; he also commanded 5th Corps) to launch a flanking attack on the rear of the 5th Division; although the Chinese were unable to recover lost ground, these attacks, conducted in early March, slowed down the Japanese advance considerably. Notorious for its poor disciplinary record and frequent insubordination, the 3rd Army Group consisted largely of poorly equipped Sichuan provincial troops, many still wearing tropical dress and straw sandals. Having marched all the way from

These Japanese artillerymen are eating a meal besides their 7.5cm field gun (either a Type 41 or its successor, the Type 95) and its limber. This picture was taken in Shandong during the Japanese drive south towards Tai'erzhuang. One key factor in Japan's favour during the early part of the Second Sino-Japanese War was the Japanese quantitative and qualitative superiority in field guns. Even so, all Japanese artillery units of this era and even towards the end of the conflict remained dependent upon horse power as the main means of transport. (The Asahi Shimbun via Getty Images)

south-western China, some 1,500km away, to fight in northern China, they encountered bitterly cold winter conditions. They were the poorest of the poor, despised and ridiculed, but their dogged fighting performance in the Xuzhou campaign would stun many.

After the capture of Jinan, Isogai spread the bulk of his forces along the Jinan–Qingdao railway and dispatched the Katano Detachment (Col Katano Sadami with 1½ battalions of infantry from the 21st Infantry Regiment and a mountain battery) to clear the Chinese from his southern flank. Commencing on 21 February, Katano's southerly drive was blunted at Ju County, a small town 170km north-east of Linyi city, itself approximately 80km north-east of Tai'erzhuang. Responsible for Linyi's defence was the depleted 40th Corps (Maj-Gen Pang Bing-xun) with only one division, the 39th (Lt-Gen Ma Fa-wu). Despite the Chinese lack of heavy weapons (the whole corps had only four field guns), Pang halted the Japanese advance on 21–22 February. Isogai ordered Maj-Gen Sakamoto Jun to aid Katano with his 21st Infantry Brigade (21st and 42nd Infantry regiments), supported by one field-artillery battalion and one mountain-artillery battery; on 24 February the two forces were designated the Sakamoto Detachment, and that officer took command of Katano's contingent as well as his own.

To save Pang from collapse, on 17 February Li sent Zhang's 59th Corps, which had just been redeployed from blocking the 13th Division at the Huai River. At dawn on 14 March, Zhang directed his entire corps across the Yi River and hit Itagaki on the western flank, while Pang dispatched the 39th Division's 115th and 116th Infantry brigades on a hasty march on the Japanese eastern flank, bypassing the forward enemy troops and hitting the Japanese in the rear. With both flanks under threat, Sakamoto withdrew to Ju County on 29 February. Zhang was ordered to pursue, but the Japanese counter-attacked on 19 March, this time supported by aircraft from the Provisional Air Corps. Without any anti-aircraft countermeasures, the Chinese were yet again forced to retreat and fight a rearguard battle until aid from the 333rd Infantry Brigade (111th Division, 57th Corps), as well as a cavalry regiment from 13th Corps (Lt-Gen Tang En-bo), arrived on 29 March to stabilize the situation.

To the west, Isogai's drive south from Jinan was spearheaded by two detachments, led by Maj-Gen Nagase Takehira and Maj-Gen Seya Hajime. Newly promoted and mentored by his predecessor, Maj-Gen Tajima Eijiro, Nagase led his brigade group (4½ infantry battalions and two artillery battalions, supported by tanks) to take Yanzhou (formerly known as Chiyang/Tzuyang) on 4 January. Following the Beijing–Nanjing railway line, from there Nagase branched off to the west towards the Grand Canal to take Jining on 11 January and crossed the canal to take Jiaxiang on 25 February. This drive west was to protect the 10th Division's western flank, and the two-pronged attack also helped to keep the Chinese guessing which was the main thrust. Like Katano's force, the 10th Division encountered fierce resistance. Provisional Chinese troops of the 22nd Division (55th Corps) and 127th Division (45th Corps) attacked from the west, trying to sever Isogai's southwards advance and to recover lost ground – including Qufu, the home of the Chinese sage Confucius. Despite their bravery and determination, the Chinese could not overcome superior Japanese firepower, although minor Chinese victories were still possible using ambush and hit-and-run tactics.

While Nagase was battling the Chinese around Jiaxiang, Jining, Yanzhou and Qufu, a second Japanese force heavily supported by air power continued the southward drive. Commanded by Maj-Gen Seya Hajime, this force included: the 10th and 63rd Infantry regiments (the 10th Infantry Regiment at half-strength); the 10th Field Artillery Regiment (one battalion only), the 2nd Heavy Artillery Regiment (one battalion), the 3rd Battalion, CGA Artillery Regiment (less one battery) and two temporary artillery batteries (one mountain, one field); the 10th Independent Machine Gun Company; one independent reconnaissance company; the 10th and 12th Independent Armour companies; and miscellaneous support troops (transport, engineers, etc.).

Seya's force departed from Zoucheng City (formerly Zou County) on 14 March, but met heavy resistance on the outskirts of Teng County (now Tengzhou City). This key town was defended by Sichuan provisional troops of 41st and 45th corps, serving in the 22nd Army Group (Lt-Gen Sun Zhen). Like many Chinese formations at the time, this was a depleted force, fielding only two divisions'-worth of troops. Knowing these provisional troops were poorly armed, Gen (1st Grade) Li Zong-ren boosted the force with additional weapons, most importantly 800 crates of grenades – 40,000 bombs.

The commander of Teng County was Maj-Gen Wang Ming-zhang, GOC 122nd Division and temporary forward field commander of 41st Corps. Wang placed his first line of defence some 18km north of Teng County; it was defended by the 125th Division, supported by the 127th Division,

Both the Communists and Nationalists recruited a number of female soldiers during the war. While many worked in rear-echelon roles as medics and signallers, there were also some who fought in the front line as infantry, or carried out reconnaissance work – as well as in a spying role, in which many excelled. According to records, by 1944–45, about 10 per cent of the Chinese Army (not including the Communist force) was female. Although it was rare, some disguised themselves as male and served in all-male units, only to be exposed after capture or when invalided out. (Evergreen Photos)

which was tasked with conducting guerrilla warfare to slow down the Japanese advance. The second and final line of defence was manned by the 124th Division (Lt-Gen Sun Zhen), with the 372nd Infantry Brigade inside the city centre and the 370th Infantry Brigade outside the city walls to protect the western flank. Supporting the 124th Division was the 364th Infantry Brigade (122nd Division) deployed around Jiehe and tasked with fighting a withdrawing battle to within the city; the rest of the 122nd Division was held in reserve.

Despite the overwhelming superiority of Seya's force, the Chinese layered defence slowed the Japanese advance to a snail's pace. To get his troops' progress back on schedule, Seya split his force into two, one element to attack Teng County and the other to head towards Tai'erzhuang. The 63rd Infantry Regiment proceeded south, leaving the 10th Infantry Regiment to capture the walled city. On 16 March, Japanese forces breached the ancient wall after a 30-gun bombardment that lasted most of the day. Inside the city were ten companies'-worth of Chinese troops; many were rear-echelon personnel and regimental police who lacked heavy weapons. Waves of Japanese rushed the breach, but were beaten back with a deluge of grenades amid close-quarter combat with bayonets and scimitars. Backed up by armour, the Japanese finally took Teng County by 1200hrs on 18 March. Chinese casualties were extremely heavy, with the 22nd Army Group estimating that it lost half of its troops; 80 per cent of the city's defenders were killed. Part of the reason was that many of the injured defenders chose self-immolation instead of being taken prisoner; the Japanese attitude to captured Chinese personnel was already notorious. Of the 10,000 Chinese casualties, only 29 were captured alive, but all were summarily killed, two by Lt-Gen Isogai himself. In the mass of dead Chinese personnel lay Major Lu Qing-fu, formerly a staff officer

SHUMATE
2018

The fight for Teng County

During the 1930s, many Chinese cities and towns were still protected by ancient walls. The Japanese blasted their way through to Teng County, but were met by a ferocious counter-attack from the 372nd Infantry Brigade. These provincial troops from Sichuan in south-west China were often ridiculed by the rest of the Chinese Army. Many were opium addicts, a habit left over from the warlord days; the opium pipe is known in China as the opium 'gun', thus these troops were known as the 'two guns soldiers'. Poorly equipped (some even still wearing straw sandals), and even poorer in discipline, they nevertheless made up for their deficiencies by their bravery and determination to fight, often to the last man. During this period in the late 1930s, many Chinese provincial troops still had a huge scimitar slung across their back, making this one of the last engagements where medieval-era weapons were pitted against 20th-century firearms. This picture shows the charge of the Sichuan troops in a counter-attack against the recently breached section of the city wall. Despite their initial success, the Chinese were defeated by the superior firepower of the Japanese and Teng County was captured by Maj-Gen Seya Hajime's men.

in the 364th Infantry Brigade (122nd Division), who survived the butchery. Rescued by the locals, he was nursed back to health and miraculously rejoined the NA to fight again in the battle of Wuhan. Despite the heavy Chinese casualties, the dogged defence of this insignificant town bought the Chinese five valuable days in which to beef up the defence of Tai'erzhuang; without this respite, the course of the entire war could have swung the other way.

By 19 March, the advance guard of the 63rd Infantry Regiment (Col Fukue Shinpei), having bypassed Teng County, had taken Lin City (17 March) and reached Hanzhuang. Tai'erzhuang was ready to face the Japanese onslaught as the 2nd Army Group (Gen Sun Lian-zhong) had arrived. Normally, the 2nd Army Group consisted of two corps, but it had taken heavy casualties during the defence of Niangzi Pass in 1937 and had not recovered fully, and fielded only three divisions (the 30th, 31st and 27th). Sun placed the 31st Division in Tai'erzhuang. Maj-Gen Chi Feng-tian, GOC 31st Division, placed the 184th Infantry Regiment inside the city, protected by its ancient walls. Outside were the 181st, 182nd and 183rd Infantry regiments, placed on the eastern, western and northern flanks respectively. Because of the successful delaying tactics employed at Teng County, Sun's men had ample time to construct solid defences, all with at least 1m of overhead cover.

Fukue was ordered to secure the Grand Canal line near Hanchuang and Tai'erzhuang, place garrisons in Lin City and Yi County, north of Tai'erzhuang, and then support the operations of 5th Division. On 23 March Seya dispatched a detachment (Lt-Col Kamura Asahi – one infantry battalion, one armoured-car company, one field-artillery battery and one mountain-artillery battery) from Lin City to Linyi to support the 5th Division. On 24 March, Seya launched his attack on Tai'erzhuang with a relatively weak force – only one battalion of infantry supported by one battery of artillery – not knowing Tai'erzhuang had been reinforced by the Chinese. In his eagerness to prove himself, Isogai drove his force far deeper into enemy territory than he should have. He was supposed to have waited for Ogisu's 13th Division to close in on Xuzhou from the south and Itagaki's 5th Division to pass Linyi for additional safety.

Unknown to the Japanese, elements of 20th Army Group (Lt-Gen Tang En-bo) – seven divisions (2nd, 4th, 6th, 13th, 25th, 89th and 139th) – were rapidly approaching Tai'erzhuang from the west. Not only were Tang's troops at full strength; they were also Chiang's elite, German-trained and -equipped Category One soldiers. As soon as Tang's troops had begun to arrive on 15 March, they had engaged the Japanese north of the Tai'erzhuang area. Even so, Gen (1st Grade) Li Zong-ren did not want to risk losing the Central Army's elite divisions in a direct head-to-head encounter, preferring to set a trap by luring Seya to attack Tai'erzhuang. Provided Chi's men could hold the line, Tang's forces could drive around the back of the Japanese to encircle them and give the Chinese the upper hand.

The first Japanese attack ended in dismal failure. In response, Seya beefed up his force with an additional battalion of infantry and fielded not just artillery but also air power and Type 94 tankettes. Maj-Gen Wang Bo-xiang, 2IC 27th Division, wrote in his diary of an attack mounted by ten Japanese tankettes; he witnessed a Chinese battalion commander's death, crushed by a tankette, and saw Chinese troops climb aboard the vehicles, thrusting their rifles into observation slits and putting grenades into air vents.

The Japanese managed to secure a small foothold in the north-eastern corner of the city, then another on the city's northern wall, but were unable to capitalize on their success further. By midday on 25 March, the Chinese were ready to play their trump card, for Tang had brought with him a battalion equipped with nine German 15cm sFH 18/32L howitzers, which proved to be devastating. Furthermore, caught in the confines of the narrow streets, the Japanese tanks and long-range weapons were unable to fulfil their potential. The situation called for close-quarter combat, at which the Chinese excelled. Major Wu De-hou, OC 3rd Battalion, 176th Infantry Regiment (88th Infantry Brigade, 30th Division), was tasked with forming a 'dare-to-die' squad. Armed with grenades, they hit at the tanks' vulnerable spots, their tracks, and immobilized them for easy picking later, but at a tremendous cost. Seven decades later, Wu recalled that he started with a 40-man force, of whom only three remained at the end of the battle.

On 28 March the Japanese managed to penetrate the north-western corner of the city, but could not make further progress. In contrast to the battle in Shanghai during the previous summer, these Chinese regional troops had some knowledge of urban warfare. Instead of moving through the streets, they made 'mouse-holes' in buildings and moved through the houses to close in on the Japanese. On the other hand, the Chinese were unable to dislodge the Japanese entirely.

On 25 March, the Kamura Detachment dispatched to Linyi was caught by Tang's 20th Army Group in Guoliji (at that time a small village, but in the eastern suburbs of Zaozhuang today), halfway between Lin City to the west and Linyi to the east. Hearing the news, Sakamoto decided to help to relieve Seya by attacking Tai'erzhuang, thereby drawing the Chinese away from Guoliji. On 31 March, Sakamoto dispatched four battalions of infantry supported by two battalions of field artillery towards Tai'erzhuang, but they too were caught in a trap in Huanglin Zhuang, a hamlet 6km east of Tai'erzhuang, on 2 April. Trapped and losing the will to fight, the Japanese soon succumbed to a sense of panic that migrated through the ranks, and Chi's men were able to recover the areas taken by the Japanese in both their north-eastern and north-western penetrations. On 5 April, Isogai ordered

This group of Japanese soldiers are breaching a wall in a Chinese township during the Japanese advance into Tai'an in the north of Shandong province on the way to Tai'erzhuang. In the early days of the Second Sino-Japanese War, neither side was very skilled in fighting in built-up urban environments. It was not until Tai'erzhuang that the Chinese were able to develop and apply such skills, moving between buildings rather than via streets and other open areas. (adoc-photos/Corbis via Getty Images)

a total withdrawal from Tai'erzhuang. In the midst of the retreat, the IJA's heavy-artillery units were trapped by fast-approaching Chinese and many of the guns had to be abandoned.

For the first time since 1937, the Chinese were able to inflict on the Japanese a hammering so great that they had to withdraw. The Chinese resistance at Tai'erzhuang was so determined that it was acknowledged by the Japanese. The war diary of the IJA's 10th Infantry Regiment recorded that although the Japanese tried to persuade the Chinese to surrender, they refused to do so; the dead were piled thickly in the trenches, leading the Japanese to pay tribute to their enemy's bravery and heroism. The Chinese propaganda machine went into overdrive, exaggerating the losses inflicted on the Japanese (actual deaths were in the region of 5,800, but the propaganda figure was more like 20,000), but this 'victory' greatly enhanced Chinese morale. While we have no accurate figure for overall Chinese casualties, by using figures from the engagement at Teng County – 122nd Division casualties in excess of 50 per cent (1,500+), compared with 142 sustained by the 1st and 3rd battalions, 10th Infantry Regiment, which spearheaded the Japanese assault – we can guess at how mismatched the two armies were. While it is arguable that the Chinese forces at Teng County were second-rate provincial troops, even if the best Chinese units had been involved, Chinese casualties might have been reduced from 10:1 to 2:1 or 3:1 in the Japanese force's favour.

Despite this temporary setback, the IJA responded with a revitalized and much-reinforced effort, not only halting any Chinese advance but launching a counter-attack that eventually led to the Japanese capture of Xuzhou on 19 May. Unlike the battle of Shanghai in 1937, the Chinese were able to withdraw in good order and the Xuzhou campaign bought the Chinese some time, allowing Chiang to defend Wuhan properly.

Wanjialing

23 July–17 October 1938

BACKGROUND TO BATTLE

Just before the fall of Nanjing in December 1937, the Chinese Government managed to decamp to Chongqing, deep in the south-west, which remained the nation's capital until 1945. While Chongqing was formally the new capital of China, in practice Wuhan was where the country's civil servants operated. It was because of the isolation and its relative inaccessibility that the nation's administration, as well as the bulk of Chiang's army, was still holed up in Wuhan. Wuhan was convenient not only because it was centrally located, but also because it was the nexus of the rail, road and waterways transport networks – the endpoint of vital lifelines to the outside world. From Hong Kong in the south came vital military supplies from the West and from the north-west came Soviet military aid. Wuhan was also home to a small but vital force, the Soviet Volunteer Group, which during 1937–41 constituted the only effective and viable air power until new Chinese pilots could be trained. It was all that Chiang had as an air force.

On 19 May 1938, the Japanese took Xuzhou, but it was a pyrrhic victory; the IJA failed to achieve its aim, to destroy Chinese forces around Xuzhou, and the Chinese managed to escape westwards in good order. Fielding 20,000 men plus tanks, the IJA's 14th Division, the vanguard of the NCAA's I Corps, charged down from the north and across the Yellow River – again against orders – to try to intercept the fleeing Chinese. The location of the crossing was sufficiently close to Zhengzhou, the capital of Henan province, some 390km west of Xuzhou. Zhengzhou was a vital staging point on the Beijing–Wuhan railway; capture of the city would allow the IJA to march down the railway line to reach Wuhan, bypassing the Dabie Mountains, a formidable obstacle to the north-east of Wuhan. The Chinese tried to surround the over-extended 14th Division in what became known as the battle of Lanfeng, but the lucky Japanese were saved by the incompetence and disobedience of a few Chinese commanders who failed to close the trap, thus allowing the 14th Division to escape annihilation.

By the end of May, the Japanese imperial headquarters sensed that the land campaign was slipping out of their control and ordered the NCAA to halt all offensive operations. Like many previous orders, it was ignored; IJA forces were only 40km from Zhengzhou. In desperation, Chiang Kai-shek initiated the 'doomsday' plan, devised by his German advisors back in 1935, to use the floodwaters of the Yellow River to halt the Japanese advance to Zhengzhou. The dykes were blown, a surge of water some 1.5m high sweeping away most of the pursuing IJA forces (most of the 14th Division and part of the 16th Division). The muddy ground also prevented all movements, especially of heavy guns and equipment, halting any further Japanese operations in this area. To prevent starvation, the trapped Japanese forces had to be sustained by airdrops. While many of the troops were saved, much of their equipment – including tanks and guns – had to be abandoned.

The result was that the Japanese had to switch their main thrust from the NCAA to the CCEA. This realignment caused many delays, allowing the Chinese to shore up Wuhan's defences; but while the flooding brought military success, it was a domestic disaster for the civilians in the area. With the Chinese plan having been poorly planned and executed, many peasant farmers were caught up in the floods. Estimates range from 90,000 to as many as 500,000 deaths from disease and starvation, with 4 million made homeless, many becoming refugees.

The Wuhan campaign was essentially a rerun of the 1937 Shanghai–Nanjing campaign. The Japanese sought to force the Chinese to capitulate by destroying the NA forces in a grand pincer movement and capturing China's capital, while conducting a secondary operation in the south to capture Guangzhou (Canton), a key staging point on the Hong Kong–Wuhan railway, thereby denying the Chinese vital aid from Hong Kong. The Japanese saw the capture of Wuhan as a major step towards victory in China and in order to do this, the IJA devoted all available resources to the Wuhan campaign. By the start of the campaign in June 1938, the IJA had not only doubled in size, from 17 to 34 divisions; fully 31 of these 34 divisions – 800,000 men – were deployed in China. The Imperial Headquarters allocated 14 divisions to the Wuhan operation and three to the Guangzhou operation. Not to be left out, the IJN captured Xiamen (Amoy), using three brigades of the Special Naval Landing Force.

With the northern approach blocked, the task of capturing Wuhan was assigned to the CCEA, commanded by Gen Hata Shunroku. Hata's plan was to use XI Corps (Lt-Gen Okamura Yasuji) as the southern pincer, approaching Wuhan via the Yangtze River with the help of the IJN. Having been reassigned to the CCEA, II Corps (Lt-Gen Prince Higashikuni Narahiko) was to form the northern pincer, driving south from Xuzhou to Hefei, the capital of Anhui province, some 300km away to the south. At Hefei, II Corps was to split into two forces: one would strike west and capture Xinyang, cutting the Beijing–Wuhan railway, while the other would turn south-west, crossing the Dabie Mountains to approach Wuhan from the north-east. Crossing the mountains would mean abandoning much of the IJA's heavy weaponry and armour support, however. With the Japanese lacking these force multipliers, the fight suddenly became much more balanced.

The CCEA's attack on Wuhan commenced on 30 April 1938 with a move to capture Hefei by advancing the 6th Division across the Yangtze River while two elements of XI Corps, the 106th Division (Lt-Gen Matsuura Junrokuro) and the Hata Detachment (Maj-Gen Hata Juichi), moved down the Yangtze under the protection of IJN aviation to seize Hukou at the northern point of Lake Poyang. Consisting of men from the Taiwan Garrison, the Hata Detachment had participated in the battles of Shanghai and Nanjing under the command of Maj-Gen Shigeto Chiaki. Owing to Chinese fire from both shores, however, the Hata Detachment was forced to disembark from its transports in order to clear both river banks so the IJN could proceed. From Hukou, the Yangtze turns north-west; as the Japanese got nearer to Wuhan, they found that both sides of the river banks were covered with Chinese defensive positions, forcing the IJA forces to clear the approach in a series of protracted battles. On the southern bank of the Yangtze, around the area of the western banks of Lake Poyang, were elements of II Army Corps (Gen Zhang Fa-kui) and I Army Corps (Lt-Gen Xue Yue). Zhang's troops were responsible for the outer defence while Xue's forces were placed in depth. The IJA's XI Corps, now much reinforced and supported with naval gunfire and ground-attack aircraft, was able to capture Jiujiang and Gutang Township on the river and lake banks. To protect the southern flank of his XI Corps, Okamura ordered the capture of De'an, a vital refuelling point on the Jiujiang–Nanchang railway, but dogged Chinese defence in the area north of De'an stymied any Japanese progress. Unable to break through to De'an, the Japanese deployed chemical weapons, but were still unable to dislodge the Chinese. In order to break through, the 106th Division was sent on a risky mission across the hills west of De'an in an attempt to flank the Chinese defenders with a giant right hook. It was under these circumstances that the battle of Wanjialing was fought.

The Type 89 No. 1 (I-Go) Model B (Otsu) was one of Japan's key infantry-support tanks during the early years of the China campaign. It was designed with northern China's dry and cold climate in mind, and – unusually for tanks of that era – had an air-cooled diesel engine. Armed with a 5.7cm short-barrelled cannon, it proved to be effective against fortified positions. In the eight years of open warfare between the Japanese and Chinese, there were no recorded incidents of tank-vs-tank combat. (Keystone/Getty Images)

Wanjialing, 23 July–17 October 1938

MAP KEY

1 23 July: The Hata Detachment (Maj-Gen Hata Juichi) lands and proceeds to Jiujiang; on 30 July, it is followed by the 106th Division (Lt-Gen Matsuura Junrokuro), which proceeds to Lake Chi. During a seven-day battle, the 106th Division is badly mauled when it attempts to push south around Shahe.

2 21 August: To open a different route to De'an, the Sato Detachment (Maj-Gen Sato Shozaburo) takes Xingzi; it then tries to break through to Aikou.

3 21 August: Hata is ordered to support the 9th Division's 6th Infantry Brigade (Maj-Gen Maruyama Masao) to capture Ruichang, which falls on 24 August. Thereafter, Maruyama is ordered to proceed to Mahuiling, arriving on 3 September; he is then ordered to return to Ruichang (arriving on 8 September) to support the Hata Detachment's movement west. Hata and Maruyama eventually cross the Fu Shui River on 17–18 October.

4 15 September: The 27th Division (Lt-Gen Homma Masaharu) is ordered to leave its concentration area east of Mount Lu to take Ruoxi via Ruichang, but its progress is severely slowed by Chinese units from 13th, 18th and 32nd corps, plus the 141st, 13th (New) and 15th (New) divisions around Xiao-ao (on 17 September).

5 22 September: Having rested, the 106th Division moves to take De'an from the rear via the hills at Wanjialing. Its progress is slowed by determined attacks by 4th Corps (Lt-Gen Ou Zhen) and eventually (on 28 September) it is trapped around the hamlet of Leiminggu-liu.

6 8 October: The Saeda Detachment (Maj-Gen Saeda Yoshishige), temporarily attached to the 27th Division, is ordered to rescue the 106th Division. With Saeda unable to reach Matsuura, on 10 October, the Suzuki Detachment (Maj-Gen Suzuki Harumatsu) is rushed from Jiujiang to join Saeda. The Chinese cease combat operations on 10 October, and Japanese rescue forces manage to break through to the survivors of the 106th Division on 17 October.

7 13 October: The Chinese forces withdraw from the battlefield. In order to rapidly rebuild the strength of the 106th Division, Saeda's force is incorporated into the 106th Division while the Suzuki Detachment moves west, arriving at Xintanpu on 18 October.

Battlefield environment

Wanjialing is an area of high ground, heavily wooded for the most part and interspersed with peaks. In between these peaks are narrow patches of land where subsistence farmers make a meagre living from the terraced fields. Leading from village to village are narrow mountain footpaths suitable only for a single person and a pack animal. These pathways can also be very steep in parts, thus forcing the Japanese to switch from their usual motor vehicles to mules and horses to transport supplies. Owing to the limited weight and volume each pack animal could carry, this means that the Japanese had to leave behind all their heavy weapons and be frugal with ammunition when traversing this mountain.

With the Japanese stripped of their formidable firepower and the Chinese aided by the dense woods' suitability for close combat, the setting favoured the Chinese. Although the peaks in Wanjialing are only about 50m from the plateau floor, this was enough for gravity to come into play when small arms and hand grenades were the main weapons of the Chinese infantryman. The hills of Wanjialing are also famous for their lingering fog and mist, which the Chinese exploited to the full when laying ambushes.

To the south of Wanjialing is the Boyang River, which could be crossed in only a handful of places and formed a natural barrier against further progress towards De'an. On the other hand, the mighty Yangtze River to the north acted as the main supply route for the Japanese; at Jiujiang the Yangtze is just over 2km wide.

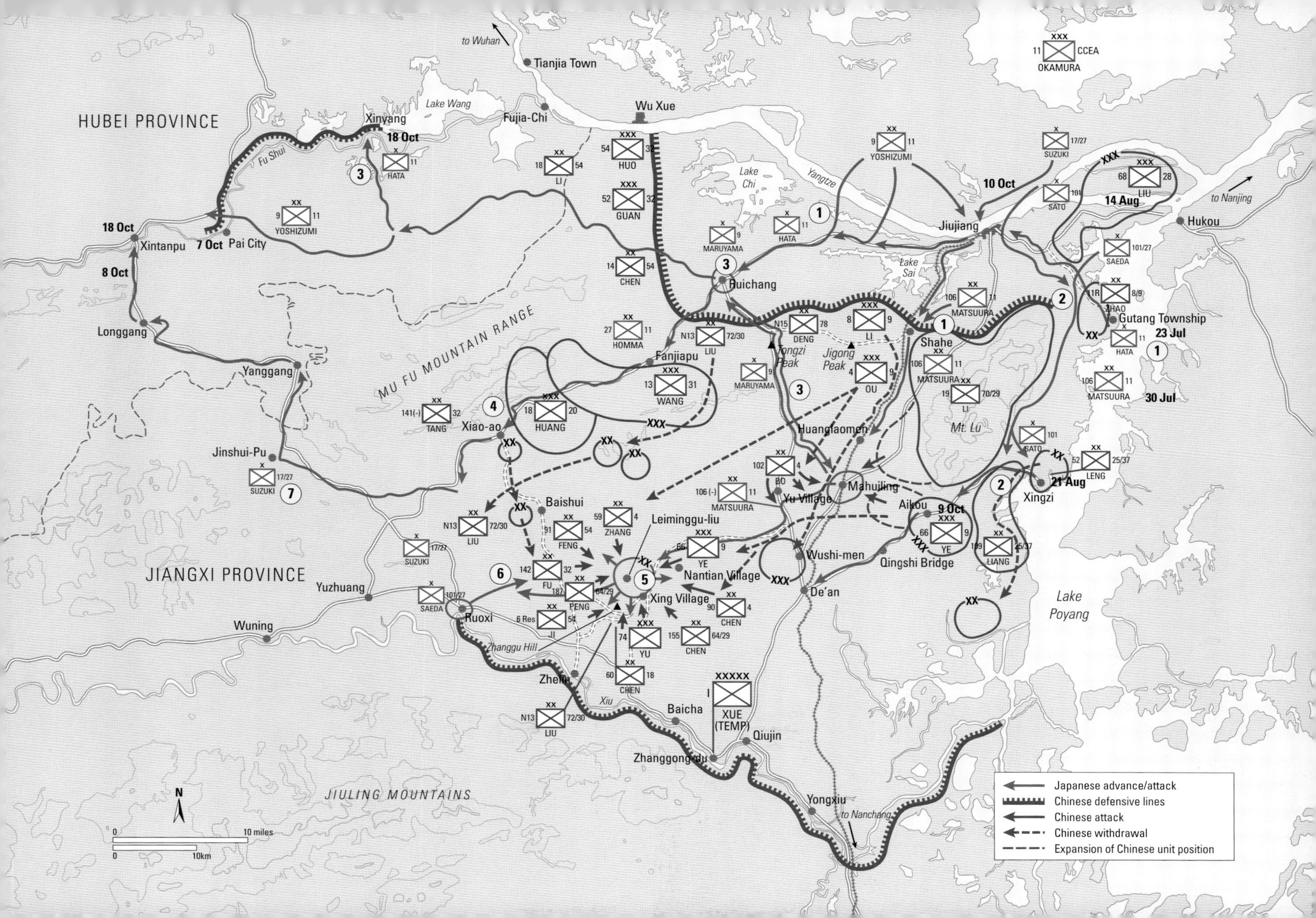
HUBEI PROVINCE
JIANGXI PROVINCE
MU FU MOUNTAIN RANGE
JIULING MOUNTAINS
to Wuhan
to Nanjing
to Nanchang
Tianjia Town
Lake Wang
Fujia-Chi
Wu Xue
Xinyang
18 Oct
Fu Shui
Xintanpu
7 Oct
Pai City
8 Oct
Longgang
Yanggang
Jinshui-Pu
Lake Chi
Yangtze
Lake Sai
Jiujiang
10 Oct
14 Aug
Hukou
Gutang Township
23 Jul
30 Jul
Ruichang
Shahe
Tongzi Peak
Jigong Peak
Fanjiapu
Xiao-ao
Huanglaomen
Mt. Lu
Xingzi
21 Aug
Mahuiling
Yu Village
Aikou
9 Oct
Qingshi Bridge
Wushi-men
De'an
Lake Poyang
Baishui
Leiminggu-liu
Nantian Village
Xing Village
Yuzhuang
Wuning
Ruoxi
Zhanggu Hill
Zhelin
Xiu
Baicha
Qiujin
Zhanggong-du
Yongxiu
OKAMURA
CCEA
YOSHIZUMI
SUZUKI
SATO
LIU
SAEDA
ZHAO
HATA
MATSUURA
MARUYAMA
HUO
GUAN
CHEN
LI
DENG
OU
HOMMA
WANG
HUANG
TANG
BO
LENG
LIANG
YE
ZHANG
FENG
FU
PENG
JI
YU
XUE (TEMP)
N
0
10 miles
10km
Japanese advance/attack
Chinese defensive lines
Chinese attack
Chinese withdrawal
Expansion of Chinese unit position

INTO COMBAT

On 20 September 1938, Lt-Gen Okamura ordered the 106th Division to advance over the hills at Wanjialing after being given information that a gap had been found in the positions of the Chinese II Army Corps. This 'gap' was created when the Chinese were forced to redeploy troops to counter the sudden appearance of the 27th Division (Lt-Gen Homma Masaharu) west of Ruichang. The 27th Division's march was halted on the road to Xiao-ao by 32nd Corps (Lt-Gen Shang Zhen). Okamura's choice for this breakthrough was the 106th Division, well rested and reinforced after suffering a mauling at Shahe (30 July–5 August). It had suffered over 8,000 casualties, including many officers: two out of three regimental commanders, six out of nine battalion commanders and half of all company and platoon commanders.

Another motivation for this Japanese venture across the hills at Wanjialing was that the 101st Division's progress to De'an was well behind schedule. A reservist unit newly raised for the China campaign, the 101st Division (Lt-Gen Ito Masaki) was supposed to undertake only 'soft jobs' as the corps reserve and to act as the rearguard; but because of the 106th Division's poor performance at Shahe, Okamura ordered the 101st Division to seek an alternative route to De'an via Aikou. The Sato Detachment (Maj-Gen Sato Shozaburo) captured Xingzi on 21 August, but despite being reinforced by the Saeda Detachment (Maj-Gen Saeda Yoshishige) the Japanese advance was held up for more than a month by Chinese forces of 25th and 66th corps in the southern foothills of Mount Lu; Ito was nearly killed when his headquarters was hit by Chinese mortar fire. The Japanese used gas, but to no avail. Yuan Ti-ming, at that

Japan's extensive use of chemical and biological weapons during the war in China was not widely known due to the tight censorship imposed on the press by the Japanese military. Cooperative journalists were given exclusive access to stories, thus boosting their newspapers' sales, but they were only allowed to write 'approved' stories. Here, the Japanese censor has stamped this picture with the mark 'Forbidden' to prevent the general public knowing that chemical warfare was being waged in China contrary to international treaty, the 1925 Geneva Protocol (to which Japan was a signatory) having banned the use and storage of chemical (principally gas) and biological weapons. (Evergreen Photos)

The use of gas as a chemical weapon in China began in earnest in 1937 during the Shanghai campaign. It was not until the Wuhan campaign in 1938, though, that the Japanese used it in large quantities in a bid to overcome dogged Chinese resistance, which had severely slowed the Japanese advance and put back the invaders' ambitious timetable. This photograph shows Japanese troops in Shanghai in the summer of 1937. Note the long Type 30 bayonet used by the Japanese, a testament to their tactical philosophy, which favoured close combat rather than the deployment of massive firepower at a distance. (The Asahi Shimbun via Getty Images)

time a young bugler with the 2nd Machine Gun Company, 304th Infantry Regiment (102nd Division, 4th Corps), recalled that he encountered poison gas that made him cry and cough; his platoon commander ordered him to soak his handkerchief in urine and cover his mouth and nose, an expedient that proved successful.

Like the 101st, the 106th Division was made up of reservists, most being demobilized conscripts from the 6th Division. Its commander, Lt-Gen Matsuura Junrokuro – also a reservist – was eager to prove himself in light of the recent fiasco. After 20 days of recuperation in Mahuiling, and more importantly boosted with battle-replacements and additional artillery in the shape of the 52nd Field Artillery Regiment (less 3rd Battalion), seconded from the 22nd Division, the 106th Division was eager to shine. Matsuura's plan was to surprise the enemy and therefore speed was of the essence.

This Chinese soldier holds a Belgian-made M1930, a version of the Browning M1918 automatic rifle. During 1933–39, the Chinese purchased 29,550 such weapons in 7.92×57mm calibre. Unlike the ZB vz. 26 light machine gun, the M1930 had a fixed barrel that could not be changed quickly in combat. China's lack of automatic weaponry during this period contributed to the Chinese failure to defeat the Japanese. Although the Germanized units had one light machine gun per section, China's regional forces had only one per platoon. (Photograph by Malcolm Rosholt. Image courtesy of Mei-fei Elrick, Tess Johnston and Historical Photographs of China Project, University of Bristol)

A large part of the upper section of the Yellow River was flooded by order of Chiang Kai-shek to impede the Japanese advance. The Japanese ground forces found that their mobility was severely impaired; cut off from their supply trains, they were forced to halt their pursuit of the Chinese. The breach of the dyke at Garden Gate or Hua Yuan Kou was a military success but a societal disaster, killing hundreds of thousands of civilians and causing considerable displacement, loss of property, famine and disease. These tragic events drove the population to support the Chinese communists, enabling them to achieve dominance in northern China, which eventually became a base allowing Mao to defeat Chiang. (Bettmann/Getty Images)

Crucially, the nature of the rugged mountain paths prevented movement by trucks and therefore heavy weapons such as artillery and ammunition had to be carried by pack animals, which the division was short of to begin with. To minimize unnecessary stores Matsuura's troops were ordered to travel in light battle order, carrying only six days' rations. The Japanese plan accounted for nine days; for the remaining three days, the troops were ordered to fend for themselves, which would involve more pillage and killing of civilians. After all, intelligence had confirmed the absence of Chinese troops in the mountains and this mission was believed to be straightforward.

On 22 September Matsuura set off for the hills with the 136th Infantry Brigade (123rd and 145th Infantry regiments) leading, followed by the 111th Infantry Brigade (147th Infantry Regiment) on the right – a total of 12,664 men, including 500 lightly wounded. To protect his rear, Matsuura left a guard force of 2,509 men (including 388 sick) at Mahuiling; another 2,967 were in Jiujiang, including 933 in the hospital, and a further 951 between Jiujiang and Mahuiling. By the morning of 26 September, the forward elements of the 106th Division were moving in a west-south-westerly direction towards Ruoxi. Progress was slow, however, hindered by poor maps and inoperable compasses on account of the high iron content of the rocks in the area.

Matsuura's force was soon detected by the 102nd Division (4th Corps). The 102nd Division's dogged harassment of the Japanese bought time to allow Lt-Gen Xue Yue to recall the 91st, 142nd, 187th and 13th (New) divisions and the 6th Reserve Division's artillery regiment to face Matsuura's troops. This force formed the Chinese western perimeter, while to the east came elements of the 4th and 348th Infantry regiments (58th Division, 74th Corps) as well as 66th Corps, and the 90th and 155th divisions, tasked with blocking any Japanese movement to the east. By 28 September, the Chinese net had closed, severing the Japanese force's last remaining link to Jiujiang. The 106th Division was now well and truly trapped.

Messages from aerial reconnaissance told Matsuura that he was off-course by some 10km. Food and ammunition were running low and the survival of Matsuura's force was only sustained by airdrops. Okamura decided to dispatch Maj-Gen Saeda Yoshishige, temporarily attached to the 27th Division, to lead a rescue force (three infantry battalions, two field batteries from the 106th Artillery Regiment and one company of tanks). Just before the Saeda Detachment was about to set off, however, it was held back to await the arrival of 2,700 replacement troops who had just landed at Jiujiang. On 8 October Saeda's force finally set off from Ruoxi.

Meanwhile, the Chinese, realizing they had the upper hand, tightened the net and poured in more reinforcements to ensure the prize could not escape. The Chinese 51st Division replaced the 58th Division, which by 6 October was down to only 500 men after facing waves of a virtual suicide attack by the Japanese 113th Infantry Regiment trying to break out. The 66th Corps (159th and 160th divisions) came from the southern slopes of Mount Lu to reinforce the eastern perimeter and initiated a series of attacks from the east to try to draw attention away from the 58th Division's tenuous situation.

At this point, the vital mission for the 51st Division, which had just relieved the 58th Division, was to seize the high ground known as Zhanggu Hill, located at the southern point of the cauldron. This high ground dominated the valley where most of the 106th Division was trapped. If Zhanggu Hill could be secured it would provide a downhill run to the heart of the 106th Division, its headquarters located in a farmhouse in Leiminggu-liu hamlet (now Liuming-gu Village), less than 1km away. To seize this high ground, Maj-Gen Zhang Ling-fu, GOC 153rd Infantry Brigade (51st Division) decided to lead a night attack with three regiments (302nd, 305th and 306th); 100 of the fittest volunteers, mainly from the 305th Infantry Regiment, were chosen to spearhead the attack.

By scaling a steep cliff, 50m in height, during the night of 7/8 October, Zhang's men were able to reach the summit undetected and seize the vital hill from the Japanese. The Japanese counter-attacked at dawn on the 8th, supported by both the 3rd and 4th Air brigades, and retook the hill, but proved unable to hold on to it as night descended, cutting off vital air support. During the next 48 hours, this hilltop changed hands five times but, despite losing most of the division – some 5,000 casualties – the Chinese held this vital ground. The desperate Japanese were also trying to break out to the west. Their main thrusts were directed at the 952nd and 949th Infantry regiments (159th Division, 66th Corps); despite sustaining significant casualties, the 159th Division held the line.

Night attack on Zhanggu Hill

Japanese view: On 7 October, the men of the IJA's 136th Infantry Brigade had been trapped in the hamlet of Leiminggu-liu for many days and despite several attempts were unable to break out from the Chinese trap. Exhausted, low on supplies and suffering from poor morale, the Japanese were surprised to find the Chinese attacking from the south, which was deemed a safe arc as it was protected by a 50m steep cliff. Led by Maj-Gen Zhang Ling-fu, the Chinese attack aimed to eliminate the trapped Japanese force in Wanjialing. When 100 Chinese came tearing through the woods in the middle of the night, it was a total shock for the exhausted Japanese. Many panicked and ran, but some stood and fought, fighting the Chinese in a series of hand-to-hand combats.

Chinese view: In mounting the attack, the Chinese scaled the cliff using vines and ropes. The southern side of Zhanggu Hill was lightly defended by the Japanese, and their sentries were not very alert. Carrying all manner of weapons, from firearms to scimitars as well as plenty of grenades, the Chinese came through the wooded hills undetected and were only discovered when they were almost on top of the Japanese sentries. In close-quarter combat under the cover of darkness, the superior Japanese firepower was negated and the Chinese, despite being poorly armed, were able to cause much havoc. The Chinese came close to seizing the headquarters of the 106th Division, but they were beaten back during the daylight hours, when the beleaguered Japanese were able to call upon air support.

Despite these counter-attacks, the noose around the Japanese continued to tighten. To diminish the Japanese advantage in firepower, the Chinese 90th and 51st divisions launched their attack after dark on 10 October. Employing stealth, the attacking force was able to approach the heart of the Japanese command centre. To distinguish their own men from those of the foe in the moonless night, the Chinese stripped to the waist and attacked with scimitars anyone wearing battle dress. At one point the 51st Division's raid into the

This group of Japanese soldiers are fighting in the Wuhan campaign during the summer of 1938. The machine-gunner is operating a Type 11 light machine gun. (ullstein bild/ullstein bild via Getty Images)

Chinese troops moving through a pine forest in and around the hills at Wanjialing. These troops do not have helmets, but instead wear large straw hats with wide brims, a characteristic of southern Cantonese troops who came from sunnier climates. The Chinese soldiers shown here are armed with the Hanyang-88 rifle, a licensed copy of the German Gewehr 88. With bayonet fixed the rifle was 164.5cm long, slightly shorter than the Japanese Type 38 rifle with bayonet fixed. (Popperfoto/Getty Images)

Regional troops from Canton, southern China, can easily be identified by their British-style helmets and French weapons; here, troops man an 8×50mm Hotchkiss M1914 medium machine gun. These troops lack rucksacks, instead using the rolled-up rattan bedsheet to carry personal necessities. The 8mm ammunition differed from the national 7.92×57mm standard, causing logistical headaches for supply officers. (Evergreen Photos)

Japanese camp came close to capturing Matsuura himself. The Chinese were less than 100m from the divisional headquarters. Most of Matsuura's retinue had gone; he was alone with his chief-of-staff. One Japanese prisoner claimed that Matsuura would have committed suicide had the Chinese got any closer. The desperate situation which the Japanese were facing was later described by Private First Class Nasu Ryosuke of the logistic train, who survived the battle to become a successful illustrator and author. He recalled the chaotic conditions among the Japanese defenders, and noted that thousands of horses died. Wounded and fatigued, the Japanese were forced to drink from creeks polluted by dead bodies.

The Saeda Detachment's progress to Zhanggu Hill was held up by waves of Chinese attacks mounted by the 60th Division, the 6th Reserve Division and elements of the 142nd Division. In three days the Japanese managed to advance only 10km. Okamura decided this rescue force needed to be strengthened and ordered Maj-Gen Suzuki Harumatsu to lead another detachment (three infantry battalions and two batteries of field artillery) to support Saeda. On 13 October, Suzuki's force managed to marry up with Saeda's and because of Suzuki's seniority – he was a regular soldier, while Saeda was a reservist – he assumed command of the rescue force, now known as the Suzuki Detachment. With Suzuki closing in from the west, the 51st Division in the southern portion of the cauldron was in danger of being itself encircled. Xue immediately ordered a general withdrawal. With the trap broken, the Suzuki Detachment finally reached Matsuura on 17 October.

Of the 12,664 Japanese who set off for the hills at Wanjialing, only about 1,500 came out alive. Private Nakayama, a prisoner of war from the 106th Division, stated that only 300 or so were unwounded, and that the division lost all of its guns and equipment as well as its stores and horses. Those Japanese soldiers who came out alive emerged empty-handed. So furious was the battle and so great and pitiable the slaughter, that when Maj-Gen Tang Yong-liang, GOC 141st Division, passed through Wanjialing a year after the battle, he saw thousands of Japanese graves in the area around Leiminggu-liu.

As for the remaining Japanese guard force held up at Mahuiling, they did try to rescue their comrades, but their way was blocked by the Chinese 139th Division; with the fall of Aikou to Ito's 101st Division on 6 October, Okamura felt that there was no need to risk another encirclement. The 106th Division was clearly not suitable for combat.

The failed offensive resulted in the crippling of two Japanese divisions, the 106th and 101st. Initially, they had a combined strength of over 47,000 troops; by the end there were only 17,000 left. The Chinese casualties were equally severe, however, if not even higher than those of the Japanese. Take, for example, 74th Corps, a German-trained Category One formation. The roll-call for 30 September 1938 was 18,998 all ranks. By 15 October, 9,504 were dead or missing. Among them were seven regimental commanders and 13 battalion commanders.

The successful defence of Wanjialing halted the Japanese offensive drive towards Wuhan along the southern bank of the Yangtze River, and bought invaluable time for the Chinese Government to evacuate its civilian strategic assets to Chongqing. Wuhan fell to the Japanese on 27 October 1938; this was a blow to the Chinese, but the city was abandoned in good order and further loss of lives defending the indefensible was deemed unnecessary after the loss of Guangzhou to the Japanese on 21 October.

This Chinese soldier – his high cheekbones suggest he is of northern stock – wears what was probably the most commonly seen headgear of the period, a German-style ski cap of local manufacture. For the most part, the average Chinese soldier did not have a helmet; some even wore straw hats into battle. This Chinese ski cap differed from the German version as the ear flaps could not be turned down. The fact that his collar tab has two triangular diamonds tells us that he is probably an officer of lieutenant rank. On his top breast pocket is a cloth patch giving his name, rank and unit and the appointment that he is holding. (Underwood Archives/Getty Images)

Analysis

By the early 1930s, the ultra-nationalists within Japan's military had taken control of the country and soon began to mastermind a series of unilateral actions, such as the Marco Polo Bridge Incident, without any thoughts as to the consequences. At this critical hour, poor leadership from Prime Minister Prince Konoe Fumimaro and inaction by Emperor Showa (Hirohito) failed to send a clear and unequivocal message to these violators of Imperial orders. Col Mutaguchi Renya, CO 1st Infantry Regiment, who deliberately ignored his orders, not only avoided punishment but was promoted to major-general just eight months after the fateful events. The message was clear: daring action, even if against orders, offered a sure way to win promotion. However, in Konoe's defence, his hand was hampered by the Japanese bureaucracy, for the civilian Cabinet had no authority over the military. This time-bomb was planted in 1899 when the Meiji Constitution was promulgated. Article 11 stated that the Emperor was the supreme military commander, but the constitution makes no mentioned of civilian oversight. A second time-bomb saw the unshackling of the military by Premier Field Marshal Prince Yamagata Aritomo. Yamagata ruled that two key members of the Cabinet, the Army Minister and the Navy Minister, had to be serving officers appointed by their respective high commands. At a stroke, this gave the military a veto over the formation of any future government. Furthermore, he changed the administrative procedure to allow the armed-forces ministers to promulgate laws and regulations to the military without the prime minister's acknowledgement.

Initially, the war went so well for the Japanese that it gave the impression that China would capitulate in a just a couple of months. When Gen Sugiyama Hajime, the War Minister, went to see Emperor Hirohito for his approval for the enactment of the General Mobilization order, he told the Emperor that the Japanese would beat the Chinese in only three months. Indeed, in the space of two months, with minimal losses (140 dead and 444 wounded for the Japanese; 16,700 casualties for the Chinese 29th Corps), the

This picture shows Chinese troops in marching order with bedding and provisions. The packing style with the blankets roll on the top of the backpack is very reminiscent of World War I-style webbing. Note the large scimitar on the side of the closest soldier's backpack, and the spare canvas shoes strapped on to the back of the large pack. These canvas shoes with hardening cloth sole are not of any special military pattern but of an age-old traditional design, suitable for any occasion. (Underwood Archives/Getty Images)

CGA managed to capture Beijing and Tianjin. By January 1938, the IJA not only swept aside all Chinese resistance in the north, but also routed Chiang's elite German-trained and -equipped Central Army and sacked Nanjing. The IJA saw no need to alter its strategy or its tactics.

If Japan did not plan for war in 1937, neither did the Chinese. Chiang Kai-shek knew that war would come, but he was just not prepared to have one in 1937. His Germanized army was far from ready, while the nation's military-industrial complex was in its infancy and could only produce poor copies of Western weapons. The nation was far from united. Not only were there factions within his own party, the KMT; vast areas of the country were under the control of local warlords that might or might not follow orders from Nanjing. Gen (2nd Grade) Song Zhe-yuan of 29th Corps dithered at the critical hour. Despite the overwhelming numerical superiority enjoyed by Chiang's forces in the Beijing area – estimated by Japanese intelligence as 78,300 all ranks, facing the CGA's 5,774 before Japanese reinforcements arrived – the Chinese were soundly beaten. For the Chinese, bravery alone was not enough to compensate for their poor training and antiquated equipment. Col Miyazaki Shuichi, CoS XI Corps, claimed that the average Chinese division was no match for the average Japanese battalion. To defeat the Japanese, the Chinese had to have the right leadership on the ground while employing superior strategy and tactics – as well as plenty of good fortune.

It must be remembered that the NA of this period was far from homogeneous. There were serious inter-regional politics at work. Northerners did not always see eye-to-eye with southerners. Take, for example, Lt-Gen Xue Yue of Wanjialing fame: he was a Cantonese, a southerner. It is no coincidence that the bulk of his army (9th, 54th, 66th and 78th corps) during the critical phase of the battle of Tai'erzhuang was also of Cantonese stock. In that battle, when Gen (1st Grade) Li Zong-ren dispatched 59th Corps (Lt-Gen Zhang Zi-zhong) to Linyi to save 40th Corps (Maj-Gen Pang Bing-xun), he asked Zhang more than once to confirm whether he was willing to save Pang, for during the civil-war era they were on opposite sides of the divide and Pang was nearly killed by Zhang's forces in a closely fought engagement. Despite Zhang's assurances, Sun sent Lt-Gen Xu Zu-yi, CoS Fifth War Zone, to mediate just in case tensions flared into open hostility.

Devoid of artillery and other support weapons, the Chinese had to fight using only small arms, many of them second-rate. Furthermore, a lack of commonality in weaponry made logistics a nightmare, hampering Chinese combat efficiency. At this stage of the war, there were eight models of imported infantry rifle in the NA – the German Mauser Gewehr 98 and Karabiner 98k; the Czech ZH-29, vz.98/22 and vz.24; the Italian Modello 1891; the Polish Kbk wz.29; the Japanese Type 38; and the Soviet Mosin-Nagant Model 1891 – and a further nine locally made models. As the war progressed, blockade by the Japanese increasingly hindered the Chinese importation of key raw materials, which meant that local substitutes had to be found, which in turn affected the quality of locally manufactured arms. Even by 1945, this kaleidoscope of weapons within the NA did not diminish; in fact, it got worse with the influx of British and American armaments into China. In February 1945, an audit conducted on 17th Corps recorded the unit as being 18,000 strong with just 5,337 rifles: 98 were Soviet-made, 1,282 of Czech origin, 2,831 from a variety of Chinese state arsenals, 253 were captured Japanese rifles, 84 were German, 597 were American and 192 were of unknown origin.

Not all of the Chinese forces' problems were caused by hardware deficiencies; their poor combat performance was due in part to poor training. Simple soldiering tasks such as weapon maintenance were often overlooked. A 1943 report by the US Army's Captain Richardson complained that pitting in the barrel and working parts was common among the 250 carbines he received. Some even had lacked gunsights, or had them fall off during firing. To complicate matters, the average Chinese quartermaster had to maintain ammunition of many calibres, including 7.92×57mm, 7.62×54mm, 6.8×58mm, 6.5×52mm and 6.5×50mm. By comparison, the Japanese benefited from standardized weapons, a systematic training and recruitment system and a homogeneous and cohesive army.

By December 1938, the Japanese were taken aback by the tenacity of the Chinese soldiers, who would not accept defeat despite horrific casualties. Japanese casualties mounted as the war progressed. According to official records, during the Wuhan campaign (June–October 1938), XI and II corps suffered 21,886 and 9,932 casualties respectively; but Okamura's report for XI Corps listed 6,556 dead, 17,046 injured, 104,559 sick and 1,386 with infectious diseases. In June 1938 the IJA's 6th Division (XI Corps) had 2,000 cases of dysentery, and II Corps suffered a staggering 900 deaths from sickness during the Wuhan campaign. To defeat the Chinese, the hawks proposed

stronger measures, and for the first time the IJA began the uninhibited use of chemical weapons during the Wuhan campaign. To disguise the nature of these weapons they were called 'Red 1' (sneezing gas), 'Red 2' (vomiting agent/Adamsite) and 'Green agent' (CS/riot gas). The ferocity of these attacks increased, notably during the battle of Changde (2 November–20 December 1943), during which lethal mustard gas and Lewisite (blister agent) were used. In addition, the Japanese carried out the deliberate aerial bombing of civilian targets.

According to Shinto traditions, the Japanese cremated their dead on the battlefield. Some of the ashes could then be carried in a small wooden box wrapped in a white cloth worn like a necklace by a soldier being repatriated home. The names of the dead were entered into the controversial Yasukuni Shrine in Tokyo, which continues to commemorate all Japanese war dead since the late 19th century. In contrast, the Chinese preferred to bury their dead. (Bettmann/Getty Images)

At the beginning of 1938 the Chinese changed their strategy and began to use time and space as a means of attrition to wear down the Japanese. This strategy was successful. For the duration of the war, Japan had to devote the bulk of her resources to fighting in China. In 1941, 65 per cent of the IJA (1.38 million men) was in China as compared to 7 per cent devoted to the South East Asia campaign. Even in August 1945, China was still the focus of Japanese effort, consuming 54 per cent of the military budget. If the Chinese had not fought on despite horrific casualties, and just a fraction of this 1.38 million-strong force had been committed to Burma or the Soviet border, things might have turned out very differently for the Allies.

Gen Chen Cheng, the overall Chinese commander in the Wuhan campaign, distilled the Chinese post-mortem of the campaign into four points: (1) over-complicated command structures; (2) a lack of coordination between the services; (3) poor training and equipment; and (4) poor inter-unit cooperation and a lack of 'team spirit'. Even in peacetime, these would have been tough issues to resolve, and they continued to haunt the NA, contributing to its eventual defeat in 1949.

Aftermath

In 1937, war with China was never Tokyo's intention; it came about through a comedy of errors masterminded by a few militarist hawks. Therefore when the incident spiralled out of control there were no war strategies in place. War was profitable; as both the generals and the admirals wanted to play leading roles, this inevitably led to a divided strategy fought on two fronts, with the IJA in the north and the IJN in the centre. As the Japanese campaign drove further into the interior of China, however, the IJN lost its leadership role and the IJA once again took the lead. In May 1938, in order to regain momentum, the IJN launched a third theatre in southern China by attacking Xiamen, Shantou (Swatow), Hainan Island and Guangzhou. Despite protests by the IJA, the attack on Hainan went ahead. In addition, the IJA and the IJN both launched massive aerial bombing campaigns aimed at civilian targets, including the provisional Chinese capital, Chongqing, as well as other major cities.

Meanwhile, the Cabinet in Tokyo tried to sue for peace by seeking support from a Chinese collaborator – Wang Jing-wei, a former Chinese prime minister and No. 2 in the KMT, who headed a puppet government in Nanjing from March 1940 – to govern what the Japanese termed a 'liberated area'. In the midst of the battle, Chiang Kai-shek sent a secret emissary to explore the possibility of a ceasefire, but the hawks in Tokyo decided to toughen the already harsh terms, something that Chiang could not accept. In the meantime, the Imperial Headquarters tried to halt further expansion of the war and concentrate on consolidating 'liberated areas', but like so many previous orders, all such instructions were ignored and the war continued to expand ever deeper into China. The ferocity with which the Second Sino-Japanese War was conducted by the Japanese was profoundly out of step with the actions of the government. For the duration of the war, until the end of hostilities in September 1945, the entire Japanese war strategy and the fate of the country itself would be dictated by a few middle-ranking hotheads.

A Japanese guard in Wuhan, China's administrative capital, after it fell to Japanese forces in 1938. The large Chinese characters read (right to left), 'Wuhan Temporary HQ', while the smaller characters on the top read (right to left), 'The Chairman of the Military Committee, Nationalist Government of China'. Chiang maintained a total of 12 temporary headquarters across the country. The 12-pointed white sun on a blue background was the Chinese national emblem from 1928 to 1949. (adoc-photos/Corbis via Getty Images)

After the fall of Wuhan, Okamura's army continued to march south. On 27 March 1939, Nanchang fell to the Japanese, but at a cost. Once again it was Lt-Gen Xue Yue who wielded the punch. After almost two years of being on the back foot, Chiang launched a series of counter-attacks. Twice in the year, the Japanese were beaten, first in the battle of Suizao (20 April–24 May 1939) and then at Changsha (17 September–6 October 1939). On both occasions, it was Xue Yue who was the hero of the hour. This was to be the first of four battles of Changsha. Victory in the first three went to the Chinese, but in 1944 Changsha was lost when Lt-Gen Zhang De-neng abandoned his position against a direct order from Xue. Zhang was charged with incompetence and desertion in the face of the enemy, and executed on 25 August 1944.

ORDERS OF BATTLE

Marco Polo Bridge Incident, 7–30 July 1937

Chinese

29th Corps (Gen (2nd Grade) Song Zhe-yuan)
37th Division (Lt-Gen Feng Zhi-an; three brigades)
38th Division (Lt-Gen Zhang Zi-zhong; three brigades)
132nd Division (Lt-Gen Zhao Deng-yu; two brigades)
9th Cavalry Division (Lt-Gen Zheng Da-zhang; two brigades)
25th Independent Brigade (Maj-Gen Ling Yun-di)
26th Independent Brigade (Maj-Gen Li Zhi-yuan)
27th Independent Brigade (Maj-Gen Shi Zhen-gang)
28th Independent Brigade (Maj-Gen Cai Jian-rui)
30th Independent Brigade (Maj-Gen Yuan Xuan-wu)
Special Duties Brigade (Maj-Gen Sun Yu-tian)
Hebei PPC (Col Shi You-san)
Training Regiment (Col Dong Sheng-tang)

Japanese

China Garrison Army (Maj-Gen Tashiro Kanichiro, replaced on 12 July 1937 by Lt-Gen Katsuki Kiyoshi)
CGA Infantry Brigade HQ (Maj-Gen Kawabe Masakazu; five companies)
1st Infantry Regiment (Col Mutaguchi Renya; four battalions)
2nd Infantry Regiment (Col Kayashima Takashi; three battalions)
CGA Artillery Regiment (Col Suzuki Yorimichi; two batteries)
CGA Armour Company (24 Type 89 tanks and Type 94 tankettes)
CGA Aviation Regiment (18 aircraft)

Reinforcements, 26–30 July 1937
20th Division (Lt-Gen Kawagishi Bunzaburo; two brigades)
1st Independent Mixed Brigade (Maj-Gen Sakai Koji)
11th Independent Mixed Brigade (Lt-Gen Suzuki Shigeyasu)
Provisional Air Corps (Lt-Gen Baron Tokugawa Yoshitoshi; ten squadrons)

Tai'erzhuang, 14 March–8 April 1938

Chinese

Fifth War Zone (Gen (1st Grade) Li Zong-ren)

2nd Army Group (Gen Sun Lian-zhong)
30th Corps (Lt-Gen Tian Zhen-nan): 30th Division (Lt-Gen Zhang Jin-Zhao; two brigades); 31st Division (Maj-Gen Chi Feng-tian; two brigades)
42nd Corps (Lt-Gen Feng An-bang): 27th Division (Lt-Gen Huang Qiao-song; two brigades); 44th Independent Brigade (Maj-Gen Wu Peng-ju)

20th Army Group (Lt-Gen Tang En-bo)
52nd Corps (Lt-Gen Guan Lin-zheng): 2nd Division (Maj-Gen Zheng Dong-guo; two brigades); 25th Division (Lt-Gen Zhang Yao-ming; two brigades); 4th Artillery Regiment
75th Corps (Lt-Gen Zhou Yan): 6th Division (Lt-Gen Zhang Qi); 139th Division (Lt-Gen Huang Guang-hua)
85th Corps (Lt-Gen Wang Zhong-lian): 4th Division (Lt-Gen Chen Da-qing); 89th Division (Lt-Gen Zhang Xue-Zhong)
Army-group troops: 13th Division (Lt-Gen Wu Liang-chen; detached from the 3rd Army Group); 9th Cavalry Division; 7th Artillery Regiment; 10th Artillery Regiment; 13th Cavalry Regiment

3rd Army Group (Maj-Gen Pang Bing-xun)
40th Corps (Maj-Gen Pang Bing-xun): 39th Division (Lt-Gen Ma Fa-Wu; two brigades); Reinforcement Regiment (Col Li Zhen-qing)
59th Corps (Lt-Gen Zhang Zi-zhong): 38th Division (Lt-Gen Huang Wei-wang); 180th Division (Lt-Gen Liu Zhen-san)
Army-group troops: Cavalry regiment; 333rd Infantry Brigade (Maj-Gen Wang Zhao-zhi; detached from 111th Division, 57th Corps); 21st Division (Lt-Gen Li Xian-zhou); 9th Cavalry Division (Lt-Gen Zhang De-shun)

22nd Army Group (Lt-Gen Sun Zhen)
41st Corps (Lt-Gen Sun Zhen): 122nd Division (Maj-Gen Wang Ming-zhang); 124th Division (Lt-Gen Sun Zhen)

Straw hats are a telltale sign that these soldiers are from China's regional forces, and not members of the Central Army. They are most probably from southern or south-west China, where the climate is warmer and sunnier. The man in the front has a longish magazine pouch, probably for the Thompson submachine gun, which helps to date this photograph to sometime after 1941, when US aid began to reach China. This photograph was taken at a passing-out parade of new recruits from somewhere in south-west China, attended by foreign journalists. (Photograph by Malcolm Rosholt. Image courtesy of Mei-fei Elrick, Tess Johnston and Historical Photographs of China Project, University of Bristol)

45th Corps (Lt-Gen Deng Xi-hou): 125th Division (Lt-Gen Chen Ding-xun); 127th Division (Lt-Gen Chen Li)

First War Zone (Gen (1st Grade) Cheng Qian)
3rd Army (Gen (2nd Grade) Yu Xue-zhong)
55th Corps (Lt-Gen Cao Fu-lin): 22nd Division (Lt-Gen Gu Liang-min)

Japanese

North China Area Army (Gen Count Terauchi Hisaichi)
II Corps (Lt-Gen Nishio Toshizo)
10th Division (Lt-Gen Isogai Rensuke)
33rd Infantry Brigade (Seya Detachment; Maj-Gen Seya Hajime): 10th and 63rd Infantry regiments; 10th Field Artillery Regiment; 2nd Heavy Artillery Regiment; ad hoc artillery regiment; China Garrison Artillery Battalion; 10th Independent Machine Gun Battalion; 10th Independent Reconnaissance Company; 10th and 12th Independent Armour companies (34 Type 94 tankettes)
8th Infantry Brigade (Nagase Detachment; Maj-Gen Nagase Takehira): 39th Infantry Regiment (4½ infantry battalions); 2nd Field Artillery Battalion

5th Division (Lt-Gen Itagaki Seishiro)
21st Infantry Brigade (**Sakamoto Detachment**; Maj-Gen Sakamoto Jun): 11th, 21st and 42nd Infantry regiments; 5th Artillery Regiment
21st Infantry Regiment (**Katano Detachment**; Col Katano Teiken): 1½ infantry battalions and one mountain battery

Provisional Air Corps (Lt-Gen Baron Tokugawa Yoshitoshi)

Central China Expedition Army (Gen Hata Shunroku)
13th Division (Lt-Gen Ogisu Rippei)

Wanjialing, 23 July–17 October 1938

Chinese

Ninth War Zone (Gen Chen Cheng)

I Army Corps (Lt-Gen Xue Yue)

9th Army Group (Lt-Gen Wu Qi-wei)
4th Corps (Lt-Gen Ou Zhen): 59th Division (Lt-Gen Zhang De-neng); 90th Division (Lt-Gen Chen Kan); 102nd Division (Maj-Gen Bo Hui-zhang)
8th Corps (Lt-Gen Li Yu-tang): 3rd Division (Lt-Gen Li Yu-tang); 11th Reserve Division (Lt-Gen Zhao Ding-chang)
66th Corps (Lt-Gen Ye Zhao): 159th Division (Lt-Gen Tan Sui); 160th Division (Lt-Gen Hua Zhen-Zhong)
74th Corps (Lt-Gen Yu Ji-shi): 51st Division (Maj-Gen Wang Yao-wu); 58th Division (Lt-Gen Feng Sheng-fa)

29th Army Group (Lt-Gen Li Han-hun)
64th Corps (Lt-Gen Li Han-hun): 155th Division (Lt-Gen Chen Gong-xia); 187th Division (Maj-Gen Peng Lin-sheng)
70th Corps (Lt-Gen Li Jue): 19th Division (Lt-Gen Li Jue)

20th Army Group (Lt-Gen Shang Zhen)
18th Corps (Maj-Gen Huang Wei): 60th Division (Maj-Gen Chen Pei)
32nd Corps (Lt-Gen Shang Zhen): 139th Division (Maj-Gen Li Zao-ying); 141st Division (Maj-Gen Tang Yong-liang); 142nd Division (Maj-Gen Fu Li-ping)

II Army Corps (Gen Zhang Fa-kui)

30th Army Group (Maj-Gen Wang Ling-ji)
72nd Corps (Maj-Gen Wang Ling-ji): 13th (New) Division (Col Liu Ruo-bi); 14th (New) Division (Maj-Gen Fan Nan-xuan)
78th Corps (Lt-Gen Zhang Zai) 15th (New) Division (Maj-Gen Deng Guo-zhang); 16th (New) Division (Maj-Gen Chen Ling-ji); 43rd Division (Lt-Gen Zhou Xiang-chu); 6th Reserve Division (Col Ji Zhang-jian)

31st Army Group (Lt-Gen Tang En-bo)
13th Corps (Lt-Gen Wang Zhong-lian): 23rd Division (Maj-Gen Li Bi-fan); 110th Division (Col Wu Shao-zhou); 128th Division (Lt-Gen Wang Jing-zai)

37th Army Group (Lt-Gen Wang Jing-jiu)
25th Corps (Lt-Gen Wang Jing-jiu): 52nd Division (Maj-Gen Leng Xin); 109th Division (Maj-Gen Liang Hua-sheng)

32nd Army Group (Lt-Gen Guan Lin-zheng)
52nd Corps (Lt-Gen Guan Lin-zheng): 2nd Division (Maj-Gen Zheng Dong-guo); 25th Division (Lt-Gen Zhang Yao-ming)
54th Corps (Lt-Gen Huo Kui-zhang): 14th Division (Maj-Gen Chen Lie); 18th Division (Lt-Gen Li Fang-chen); 43rd Division (Lt-Gen Zhou Xiang-chu); 6th Reserve Division (Col Ji Zhang-jian)

Fifth War Zone (Gen (1st Grade) Li Zong-ren)

IV Army Corps (Gen Li Pin-xian)

28th Army Group (Lt-Gen Liu Ru-ming)
68th Corps (Lt-Gen Liu Ru-ming): 119th Division (Maj-Gen Tian Wen-qi); 143rd Division (Maj-Gen Li Zeng-zhi)

Japanese

Central China Expedition Army (Gen Hata Shunroku)

XI Corps (Lt-Gen Okamura Yasuji)
6th Division (Lt-Gen Inba Shiro)
9th Division (Lt-Gen Yoshizumi Ryosuke)
101st Division (Lt-Gen Ito Masaki)
106th Division (Lt-Gen Matsuura Junrokuro)
Hata Detachment (Maj-Gen Hata Juichi)
27th Division (Lt-Gen Homma Masaharu)
Saeda Detachment (Maj-Gen Saeda Yoshishige; detached from 101st Division)
Suzuki Detachment (Maj-Gen Suzuki Harumatsu; detached from 17th Division)

CCEA Air Group (Lt-Gen Baron Tokugawa Yoshitoshi): 3rd Air Brigade (Maj-Gen Chiga Chuji); 4th Air Brigade (Maj-Gen Fujita Tomo)

FURTHER READING

There is a large and growing body of scholarship on the Second Sino-Japanese War available in Chinese and Japanese, but for reasons of space we have listed only English-language studies here.

Auer, J.E.A., ed. (2006). *Who Was Responsible? From Marco Polo Bridge to Pearl Harbor*. Tokyo: Yomiuri Shimbun.

Crowley, James B. (2015). *Japan's Quest for Autonomy: National Security and Foreign Policy, 1930–1938*, Princeton, NJ: Princeton University Press.

Dom, F. (1974). *The Sino-Japanese War, 1937–41: From Marco Polo Bridge to Pearl Harbor*. London: Macmillan.

Jowett, P.S. (2011). *Soldiers of the White Sun: The Chinese Army at War, 1931–1949*. Atglen, PA: Schiffer Military History.

Jowett, P.S. & Berger, J. (2006). *Rays of the Rising Sun, Volume 1: Japan's Asian Allies 1931–45, China and Manchukuo*. Solihull: Helion & Co.

Lary, D. (2010a). *The Chinese People at War: Human Suffering and Social Transformation, 1937–1945*. Cambridge: Cambridge University Press.

Lary, D. (2010b). *Warlord Soldiers: Chinese Common Soldiers 1911–1937* (Contemporary China Institute Publications). Cambridge: Cambridge University Press.

MacKinnon, S.R. (2008). *Wuhan 1938: War, Refugees, and the Making of Modern China*. Oakland, CA: University of California Press.

Mitter, M. (2013). *The Forgotten Ally: China's World War 2, 1937–1945*. Boston, MA: Mariner Books.

Ness, L. (2015a). *Rikugun: Guide to Japanese Ground Forces 1937–1945: Volume 1: Tactical Organization of the Imperial Japanese Army & Navy Ground Forces*. Solihull: Helion & Co.

Ness, L. (2015b). *Rikugun. Guide to Japanese Ground Forces 1937–1945: Volume 2: Weapons of the Imperial Japanese Army & Navy Ground Forces*. Solihull: Helion & Co.

Ness, L. & Bin, S. (2016). *Kangzhan: Guide to Chinese Ground Forces 1937–45*. Solihull: Helion & Co.

Olsen, L. (2012). *Tai'erzhuang 1938 – Stalingrad 1942*. Miami Beach, FL: Clear Mind Publishing.

Peattie, M., Drea, E. & van de Ven, H., eds (2013). *The Battle for China: Essays on the Military History of the Sino-Japanese War of 1937–1945*. Stanford, CA: Stanford University Press.

Timperley, H.J., ed. (1938). *Japanese Terror in China*. New York, NY: Modern Age Books.

US Military Intelligence Report (28 January 1936). Statement on Commissioned Personnel Strength and Classification as to Training, China 1911–1941. Reel V, pp. 521–24.

War Area Service Corps (1946). *The Marco Polo Bridge*. National Military Council, Beijing.

A gathering of Chinese troops eating a meal. The soldier on the right has on his left sleeve a white patch bearing the letters '185D' in blue-stencilled writing, signifying that he is serving in the 185th Division. The 185th Division was formed in April 1938 by combining the remains of the 55th Division and the Wuhan garrison to defend that settlement against the advancing Japanese. On his collar is a three-triangle badge on a plain background, signifying that he is of a superior private, a rank equating to the British Army's lance corporal. (Hulton Archive/Getty Images)

INDEX

References to illustrations are shown in **bold**.